Teaching and Learning Professionalism

Report of
the Professionalism Committee

American Bar Association
Section of Legal Education and
Admissions to the Bar
August 1996

Printed and distributed courtesy of Martindale-Hubbell and
LEXIS-NEXIS, divisions of Reed Elsevier Inc.

Copyright © 1996 American Bar Association

ISBN: 1-57073-374-0

Contents

I. Introduction

A. Background

This report is the culmination of a two-year effort to determine how we can better inculcate a higher sense of professionalism among American lawyers. It should be regarded as an extension of two prior major reports issued by the American Bar Association (ABA). The first was the 1986 Stanley Commission Report promulgated by the ABA Commission on Professionalism entitled . . . *In the Spirit of Public Service: A Blueprint for the Rekindling of Lawyer Professionalism*.[1] The second is the 1992 MacCrate Commission Report which describes for the first time in a comprehensive fashion the fundamental lawyering skills and fundamental values of the profession.[2]

The ABA Section of Legal Education and Admissions to the Bar Professionalism Committee was created in 1993 by Dean Robert A. Stein who was then serving as the chair of the section. William Reece Smith, Jr., past president of the ABA and the recipient of numerous awards including the 1994 ABA Pro Bono Publico Award, was appointed the chair of the committee. The remaining members are listed in Appendix A.

The Professionalism Committee held seven meetings: September 1993 in Chicago, Illinois; January 1994 in Orlando, Florida; August 1994 in New Orleans, Louisiana; January 1995 in New Orleans, Louisiana; February 1995 in Miami, Florida; April 1995 at Notre Dame, Indiana; and August 1995 in Chicago.[3]

---

[1] This report was published in 112 F.R.D. 243 (1987) ("Stanley Commission Report").

[2] The ABA Task Force on Law Schools and the Profession: Narrowing the Gap, Legal Education and Professional Development—An Educational Continuum (1992) ("MacCrate Commission Report"). The focus of this report is on the professional values segment. *See* MacCrate Commission Report at 207–21.

[3] In addition, an exposure draft of this report was sent to approximately 30 prominent practitioners and law professors who were known to have a long-standing interest in legal ethics and professionalism. Helpful comments were received from the following individuals: Walt Bachman, Esq.; Richard E. Carter, Esq.; Professor Neil Hamilton; Professor Geoffrey C. Hazard, Jr.; Professor W. William Hodes; Robert MacCrate, Esq.; Professor Carrie Menkel-Meadow; Professor Thomas D. Morgan; Professor Deborah L. Rhode; and Professor Anthony Weiner. These comment letters were reviewed by the entire committee and most of the suggestions have been incorporated into the final draft of this report.

In addition to reviewing the recent literature on professionalism, the Committee commissioned two surveys. The first was a survey of law school ethics and professionalism courses and programs. The results of this survey are set forth in Appendix B. The second was a survey of existing professionalism programs being conducted by state and local bar associations. The results of this survey are set forth in Appendix C. A selected bibliography of books, articles, and audiovisual materials on various professionalism issues is set forth in Appendix G.

The initial charge to the Committee was "to review the role of law schools in instituting a sense of professionalism in law students during their law school studies." The Committee, early in its deliberations, determined that teaching and learning professionalism is a lifelong quest which ideally begins even before a student enters law school and continues throughout a lawyer's professional career.[4] This expansion of the Professionalism Committee's mandate has been incorporated into the Committee's recommendations.

This report represents the Committee's collective judgment of the best means to increase the level of professionalism in American lawyers. The Committee's recommendations are phrased in terms of suggestions and alternatives rather than as mandates. The choice of which of the suggestions and alternatives to implement will vary depending on the needs of the individuals or institutions that are trying to institute a professionalism program. Implementation is principally a matter of intentionality, willpower, and discipline.

B. Decline in Professionalism

In recent years there have been numerous books,[5] articles[6] and bar association reports[7] decrying a decrease in professionalism

---

[4] This is the same continuum concept adopted by the MacCrate Commission. *See* The MacCrate Commission Report, *supra* note 2, at 8.

[5] *See* Mary Ann Glendon, How the Crises in the Legal Profession is Transforming American Society 17–108 (1994); Anthony T. Kronman, The Lost Lawyer: Failing Ideals in the Legal Profession (1993); Lawyers' Ideals/Lawyers' Practices—Transformation in the American Legal Profession (Robert N. Nelson, David M. Trubek & Rayman L. Solomon, eds., 1992); Sol M. Linowitz, The Betrayed Profession: Lawyering at the End of the Twentieth Century (1994) .

[6] *See, e.g.,* Warren E. Burger, *The Decline of Professionalism*, 61 Tenn. L. Rev. 1 (1993); Geoffrey C. Hazard, Jr., *The Future of Legal Ethics*, 100 Yale L.J. 1239 (1991); Edward D. Re, *The Causes of Popular Dissatisfaction With the Legal Profession*, 68 St. John's L. Rev. 85 (1994).

[7] *See, e.g.,* Stanley Commission Report, *supra* note 1, 112 F.R.D. at 251–61; Illinois State Bar Ass'n Special Committee on Professionalism, The Bar, the Bench and Professionalism in Illinois: Proud Traditions, Tough New Problems, Current Choices (1987).

among American lawyers.[8] Although the description of the causes and symptoms vary greatly, there are six prevalent themes in these publications:

1. the loss of an understanding of the practice of law as a "calling";[9]

2. changes in the economics of the practice of law which have converted law practice from a profession to a business—making it more difficult for lawyers to devote significant amounts of time to public service activities and generating a growing sense of dissatisfaction with law practice as being incompatible with personal values and goals;[10]

3. perceived excesses of the adversarial process, including the loss of civility,[11] permitted by the existing rules governing litigation;[12]

4. an undermining of the traditional independent counseling role of lawyers;[13]

---

[8] Not everyone agrees that the level of professionalism has decreased. *See* Ronald Rotunda, *Demise of Professionalism Has Been Greatly Exaggerated*, Manhattan Law. 12 (Mr. 28, 1988).

[9] *See, e.g.*, Robert W. Gordon, *Corporate Law Practice as a Public Calling*, 49 Md. L. Rev. 255 (1990); Phoebe A. Haddon, *Education for a Public Calling in the 21st Century*, 69 Wash. L. Rev. 573 (1994).

[10] *See, e.g.*, American Bar Ass'n, THE REPORT OF "AT A BREAKING POINT," A NATIONAL CONFERENCE ON THE EMERGING CRISES IN THE QUALITY OF LAWYERS' HEALTH AND LIVES—ITS IMPACT ON LAW FIRMS AND CLIENT SERVICES (1991); Norman Bowie, *The Law: From a Profession to a Business*, 47 Vand. L. Rev. 741 (1988). The increased emphasis on billable hours as the principal criteria for compensation and evaluation of lawyers has often been singled out as the most important recent change that has undermined the capacity and willingness of lawyers to engage in *pro bono* representation and other public service activities. *See, e.g.*, Walt Bachman, LAW v. LIFE, 100–11, 137–40 (1995).

[11] *See, e.g.*, FINAL REPORT OF THE COMMITTEE ON CIVILITY OF THE SEVENTH FEDERAL JUDICIAL CIRCUIT (1992); Marvin E. Aspin, *The Search for Renewed Civility in Litigation*, 28 Val. U. L. Rev. 513 (1994); E. Norman Veasey, *Rambo Be Gone*, 4 Bus. Law Today 12 (Jan./Feb. 1995).

[12] *See, e.g.*, Andrew L. Reisman, *An Essay on the Dilemma of "Honest Abe": The Modern Day Professional Responsibility Implications of Abraham Lincoln's Representations of Clients He Believed to be Culpable*, 72 Neb. L. Rev. 1205 (1993); Murray L. Schwartz, *The Professionalism and Accountability of Lawyers*, 66 Cal. L. Rev. 669 (1978); *Symposium on the Lawyers' Amoral Ethical Role*, 1986 Am. B. Found. Res. J. 613. *See generally* David Luban, LAWYERS AND JUSTICE (1988). *But see* Jay S. Silver, *Professionalism and the Hidden Assault on the Adversarial Process*, 55 Ohio St. L. J. 855 (1994) (a spirited defense of the existing criminal law adversarial system).

[13] *See, e.g.*, David Luban, *The Noblesse Oblige Tradition in the Practice of Law*, 41 Vand. L. Rev. 717 (1988); Robert L. Nelson, *Ideology, Practice, and Professional Autonomy: Social Values and Client Relationships in the Large Law Firm*, 37 Stan. L. Rev. 503 (1985). *See also* Richard W. Painter, *The Moral Interdependence of Corporate Lawyers and Their Clients*, 67 So. Calif. L. Rev. 507 (1994).

5. concerns about the competency of lawyers and their com-
    pliance with applicable ethical codes;[14] and

6. the loss of a sense of the ultimate purpose of lawyers
    resulting from a change in the traditional concept of
    lawyers serving the public good as the intermediaries
    between the conflicting interests in our society.[15]

Suggestions for inculcating a greater sense of professionalism
in the practice of law depend in part on which of these themes is
used as the basis of the proposals. Many of the recommendations
might seem to some to be overly simplistic and based on an unreal-
istic, nostalgic vision of nineteenth-century practitioners. Others
see the suggestions for increasing the level of professionalism made
to date as having been promulgated by an elitist segment of the bar
that has a very narrow, guild view of the role of lawyers.[16] Still
other commentators have concluded that recent economic changes
in our society, largely beyond the control of lawyers, have funda-
mentally changed the practice of law.

The Committee has taken all of these themes and perspectives
into account in reaching its conclusions and recommendations. In

---

[14] *See, e.g.*, American Bar Ass'n, FINAL REPORT AND RECOMMENDATIONS OF THE
TASK FORCE ON PROFESSIONAL COMPETENCE (1983); Timothy P. Terrell & James H.
Wildman, *Rethinking Professionalism*, 41 Emory L.J. 403, 424–26 (1992).

[15] *See, e.g.*, Hazard, *supra* note 6; Geoffrey C. Hazard, Jr., *Four Portraits of Law
Practice*, 57 UMKC L. Rev. 1 (1988). *See generally* Kronman, *supra* note 5, at 11–17,
363–80 (we need to recapture the professional ideal of the lawyer-statesman).

[16] *See, e.g.*, Amy M. Mashburn, *Professionalism as Class Ideology: Civility
Codes and Bar Hierarchy*, 28 Val. U. L. Rev. 657 (1994) (civility codes reflect the
class bias views of the elitist trial bar); Ted Schneyer, *Policy Making and the Perils
of Professionalism: The ABA's Ancillary Business Debate as a Case Study*, 35 Ariz.
L. Rev., 363, 367–96 (1993) (critique of the history of what is now Rule 5.7 of the
American Bar Ass'n Model Rules of Professional Conduct).

A related theme is that it is disingenuous and unfair for lawyers who believe
that law should be practiced in an aspirational manner to criticize lawyers, who in
the course of representing their clients, may transgress one or more of the aspirational principles but not the mandatory rules which can result in disciplinary or
other sanctions. Pressuring lawyers to abide by the aspirational standards can
undermine the traditional responsibility of lawyers to represent their clients zealously to the extent authorized by law, an ancient tradition that has been particularly important in representing criminal defendants, the poor, minorities, and politically
unpopular causes. If the aspirational standards become mandatory rules, however,
then, but only then, will compliance be necessary. In other words, the rules can be
changed, but until they are, lawyers should be praised, not vilified, by fellow
lawyers, for tactics and actions that do not violate the legally enforceable rules. *See*
letter dated June 7, 1995, from Professor W. William Hodes of Indiana University
(Indianapolis) School of Law to Dean Harry J. Haynsworth, a member of the Committee. This letter is in Dean Haynsworth's file on this project. *See also* Silver, *supra*
note 12, at 857–66. *See generally* Monroe H. Freedman, LAWYERS' ETHICS IN AN
ADVERSARY SYSTEM 9–26, 113–25 (1975).

the Committee's view, the bottom line is that lawyer professionalism has declined in recent years and increasing the level of professionalism will require significant changes in the way professionalism ideals are taught and structural changes in the way law firms operate and legal services are delivered.[17] This will not be an easy task.

C. Lawyer Professionalism Defined

The designation "profession" originally applied to the clergy and practitioners of medicine and law. In modern times, profession is used to describe many specialized skills and is often simply the antonym for "amateur." In this report the definition of the professional lawyer reaches back to the traditional concept of professionalism as opposed to the modern expanded view. As one noted scholar has stated: "'Profession' comes from the Latin, *professionem*, meaning to make a public declaration. The term evolved to describe occupations that required new entrants to take an oath professing their dedication to the ideals and practices associated with a learned calling."[18]

There have been many attempts to define a profession in general and lawyer professionalism in particular. While many of these definitions have contributed to understanding (and some to misunderstanding) professionalism, perhaps nothing captures the essence of a profession better than Dean Roscoe Pound's interpretation: "pursuing a learned art as a common calling in the spirit of public service. . . ."[19]

This report expands the Pound definition and particularizes it for lawyers. The approach will be to look at the purposes of the profession, the character of the practitioner, and supportive characteristics of professionalism. In addition, the wide variety of roles of the professional lawyer in society are listed, not as part of the definition, but to demonstrate the various contexts in which the profession is practiced.

---

[17] *See*, Stanley Commission Report, *supra* note 1, 112 F.R.D. at 263–305; Robert W. Gordon & William H. Simon, *The Redemption of Professionalism?* in LAWYERS' IDEALS/LAWYERS' PRACTICES, *supra* note 5, at 230–57; Stephen Gillers, *Counselor, Can you Spare a Buck?*, 74 A.B.A.J. 80 (Nov. 1990).

[18] Deborah L. Rhode, PROFESSIONAL RESPONSIBILITY: ETHICS BY THE PERVASIVE METHOD 39 (1994).

[19] Roscoe Pound, *The Lawyer from Antiquity to Modern Times* 5 (1953). Pound's formulation was adopted by the Stanley Commission. *See* Stanley Commission Report, *supra* note 1, 112 F.R.D. at 261.

The definition developed in this report is based on "public service" being the essence of Pound's definition of a profession and "justice and the public good" being both the object of that public service and the ideal to which lawyers ought therefore be dedicated.[20] The definition of professionalism in this report concentrates on law as a combined art and science and on the professional character of those dedicated to public service.[21]

The definition of a professional lawyer adopted by this Committee is as follows: *A professional lawyer is an expert in law pursuing a learned art in service to clients and in the spirit of public service; and engaging in these pursuits as part of a common calling to promote justice and public good.*[22]

Essential characteristics of the professional lawyer are:

1.   Learned knowledge

2.   Skill in applying the applicable law to the factual context

3.   Thoroughness of preparation

---

[20] *See* Harry T. Edwards, *A Lawyer's Duty to Serve the Public Good,* 65 N.Y.U. L. Rev. 1148, 1150 (1990): ("I will argue that lawyers have a duty to conform their practices to our highest ideals—what I will call the profession's *'Public Spiritedness'* . . . In advancing a standard of 'public spiritedness,' I mean to suggest that, as part of their professional role, lawyers have a positive duty to serve the public good.")

[21] Some commentators have placed American lawyers into two categories. The first is most commonly designated as the "lawyer-statesman" or the "good lawyer." The second is the "lawyer-technician." *See* Kronman, *supra* note 5, at 2–3 (draws distinction between the lawyer-statesman who possesses the character traits of practical wisdom and good judgment and the lawyer-technician who is merely an expert in substantive and procedural law). *See also* Harry T. Edwards, *The Growing Disjunction Between Legal Education and the Legal Profession,* 91 Mich. L. Rev. 34, 66 (1992): ("A person who deploys his or her doctrinal skill without concern for the public interest is merely a good legal technician—not a good lawyer. Good lawyers are 'professional,' which means, among other things, that they are 'ethical': that they must sometimes ignore their own self-interest, or the self-interest of their clients.") This dichotomy is rejected in this report. Instead we believe that all lawyers should aspire to achieve the level of professionalism set forth in our definition of the professional lawyer, regardless of their practice setting.

[22] Some of the terms used in this definition require additional elaboration:
Professional: someone called to do essential public service that can only be done by a person with specialized knowledge.
Learned art: an art/science that requires both learned knowledge and prudential wisdom.
Common calling: a vocation requiring dedication to certain ideals as a way of life as part of a specialized group.
Public service: the performance of certain functions necessary to the general welfare or common good. This term does not refer exclusively to serving public entities or causes. A lawyer representing individual clients and zealously advocating their interests in a professional manner is engaged in public service. So is a lawyer who freely shares his or her knowledge and experience through mentoring or teaching other lawyers.

4. Practical and prudential wisdom

5. Ethical conduct and integrity

6. Dedication to justice and the public good

Supportive elements include:

1. Formal training and licensing

2. Maintenance of competence

3. Zealous and diligent representation of clients' interests within the bounds of law

4. Appropriate deportment and civility

5. Economic temperance

6. Subordination of personal interests and viewpoints to the interests of clients and the public good

7. Autonomy

8. Self-regulation

9. Membership in one or more professional organizations

10. Cost-effective legal services

11. Capacity for self-scrutiny and for moral dialogue with clients and other individuals involved in the justice system

12. A client-centered approach to the lawyer-client relationship which stresses trust, compassion, respect, and empowerment of the client.[23]

This definition defines the professional lawyer not in terms of function or characteristics but rather by the primary purpose and the characteristics of lawyers. The ideal legal profession is more than a group working with specialized skills on a job that requires expertise. It is a way of life in public service. Thus professional lawyers practice professionalism, by which we mean they embrace the characteristics or traits of the professional lawyer as we have defined that concept.

Using the definition of lawyer professionalism in this report, what is the present state of the American legal profession? Roger Cramton, former Dean of Cornell School of Law, aptly summed up

---

[23] These essential characteristics and supportive elements are also incorporated in the MacCrate formulation of the Fundamental Professional Values of the Legal Profession. *See* MacCrate Commission Report, *supra* note 2, at 140–41, 207–21.

the gap between the ideal and reality in the following excerpt from a 1985 paper he delivered in London at a plenary session of a meeting between the American Bar Association, the Senate of the Inns of Court and the Bar, and the Law Society of England and Wales:

> The disarray of the system of justice is all too apparent. The problem is not one of a lack of competence on the part of its lawyer participants, but of a lack of civilizing and moderating qualities that include accommodation, trust, compassion, and similar qualities. More competent technicians, lacking in these qualities and adhering to the total commitment model of today's codes, will multiply litigation, abuse every possible procedural device, and employ any stratagem or tactics that will help win for a client. The result is not justice but social disaster. Increasingly, many lawyers have lost a sense of obligation to courts, opponents, and the general public. . . . [T]he narrowness of the technical expert is the dominant pattern, increasing in prevalence and in official ideology.[24]

Yet if we have the will, there is time to reshape our profession so that it is more consistent with the legal professionalism we adopt in this report. Roger Cramton succinctly expressed this challenge in a 1994 law review article:

> The profession's view of itself must be reshaped in a more responsible, realistic, and truthful manner. The idealistic tradition of the profession, and especially the aspiration to balance service to client and self with regard for the interests of others, is one of the foundations on which a reshaped ethic can be built. The challenge is one of creating a new vision, courageous and truthful, of what it means to be a lawyer in today's world.
>
> I believe the major elements of a renewed vision will be:
>
> - A lawyer who cares about clients, who is accountable to them, who engages in moral dialogue with them, and who wants the legal profession to see that client interests are protected.
>
> - A lawyer who cares about equal access to justice and who strives for efficiency in the provision of legal services.
>
> - A lawyer who brings his or her moral conscience to bear on everything done as a lawyer.[25]

A somewhat different analysis of the present decline in professionalism among lawyers and a more pessimistic view of the future is expressed by Dean Anthony T. Kronman of Yale Law School:

---

[24] Roger C. Cramton, *Professionalism, Legal Services and Lawyer Competency*, in American Bar Ass'n, Justice for a Generation, 150–51 (1985).

[25] Roger C. Cramton, *Delivery of Legal Services to Ordinary Americans*, 44 Case W. Res. L. Rev. 531, 611 (1994).

[T]he profession we have inherited is not the one we joined twenty years ago. In many outward ways it is remarkably different. Its schools now encourage a style of scholarly work that is increasingly remote from—even hostile to—the concerns of practicing lawyers. Its leading firms have become giant industries, marked by an extreme division of labor and aggressive commercial tactics, that bear only a fading resemblance to their predecessors. And the caseload crisis has transformed our courts and made the work of judging a more managerial and less deliberative activity. . . .

The inward change of which I am speaking has been brought about by the collapse of the lawyer-statesman ideal. For more than a century and a half that ideal helped to shape the collective aspirations of lawyers, to define the things they cared about and thought important to achieve. Even thirty years ago, it was still a potent force in the profession. But in the years since, as my generation has risen to power, the ideal of the lawyer-statesman has all but passed from view. Law teachers no longer respect it. The most prestigious law firms have ceased to cultivate it. And judges can no longer find the time, amid the press of cases, to give its claims their due.

The ideal of the lawyer-statesman offered an answer to the question of what a life in the law should be. It provided a foundation on which a sense of professional identity might be built. And because the foundation it provided was rich in human values, this ideal was appealing at a personal level too. The decline of the lawyer-statesman ideal has undermined that foundation, throwing the professional identity of lawyers into doubt. It has ceased to be clear what that identity is and why its attainment should be a reason for personal pride. This is the great inward change that has overtaken the legal profession in my generation, and its outward manifestations, which are visible in every branch of professional life, all point to a collective identity crisis of immense—if largely unacknowledged—proportions. . . .

The likelihood that the profession as a whole will awaken to the emptiness of its condition and that there will be a great resurgence of support, at an institutional level, for the vanishing ideal of the lawyer-statesman seems to me quite low.

For the most part, I suspect, things will go on much as before, and the profession will drift more and more in the direction it has been moving this past quarter-century. Of course, each generation of lawyers makes its own contribution to the architecture of the law. The contribution mine has made has been to tear down the old system of ideas and institutions that gave the lawyer-statesman ideal its authority and power. The next, perhaps, will begin the work of rebuilding what we have torn apart. That may happen, and I hope it does, though I doubt in fact it will.[26]

---

[26] Kronman, *supra* note 5, at 353–54, 380–81.

The bottom line is that the concepts and values underlying lawyer professionalism are aspirational in nature unlike the minimum standard ethical disciplinary rules that govern lawyers' conduct. Aspirational goals are by their very nature difficult to define and even more difficult to inculcate. Nevertheless, it is our hope that the recommendations in this report will provide concrete ways to inspire and to enhance a greater sense of professionalism in American lawyers.

There are three sets of recommendations. The first deals with pre-law education. The second set concerns law school training. The third focuses on teaching and learning professionalism in the practice of law. Taken as a whole, these recommendations provide a comprehensive and interrelated system for inculcating lawyer professionalism.

II. Recommendations

A. Pre-Law School Ethics/Professionalism Training
B. Law School Professionalism Training
C. Teaching and Learning Professionalism in the Practice of Law

A. Pre-Law School Ethics/Professionalism Training

The development of a person's values and ethical beliefs does not begin with enrollment in law school. Indeed, no one can minimize the importance of the family, community, primary and secondary education, and religious institutions in this process. In an ideal world we would wish that more were done at this level to educate and develop a value system which could carry through into the legal profession. While we might, and do, encourage primary and secondary educators to adopt such programs, reality strongly suggests that our influence (and the Committee's charge) are considerably more limited than would be necessary to advocate that kind of education and development. We must leave such efforts to other persons and institutions at that level who have an interest in ethical issues.

However, once a person enters a college or university, of which most law schools in America are a part, it seems appropriate to urge that they formally adopt curricula and programs which foster an appreciation and understanding of ethical values. Systematic exposure to ethical values and issues enables students to cope more effectively in the real world regardless of their vocation or profession. We, therefore, offer three recommendations directed to colleges and universities.

In making these proposals we are not intending to be moralistic or to intrude in the education programs of undergraduate education. Rather, we believe that we have valid and viable interest in making these suggestions for two reasons.

First, we should support our undergraduate colleagues and fellow professionals in their efforts to advance education, appreciation, and student development in ethics. We should seek out colleagues in these programs who advocate improved ethical training and assist them in whatever ways we can. In doing this we also advance an understanding of ethical and professionalism issues in society generally.

Second, all law students are the products of these undergraduate, pre-professional, and professional programs. When students who have completed a solid ethical program enter a law school, they are likely to be more sensitized to the ethical and professional responsibility issues which will face them for the rest of their lives. Their further training in law school will also start at a higher plane, allowing greater development and understanding.

Our recommendations are:

1. *Each college or university should be encouraged to offer general or survey courses involving ethical and value issues and basic principles of ethical decision-making.*[27] Preferably these courses should be taken early in a student's college career. These courses should be broad in coverage so as to call students' attention to the many different situations in which ethical and value problems arise. Many people are "broad-sided" by ethical issues which they never realized that they might confront. In fact, many may not even identify the problem as an ethical issue when they are confronted by it.

In those colleges and universities where there is a distributional curriculum requirement (i.e., mandatory courses to be selected from various categories across the academic curriculum), the ethics and values offerings might be specifically listed as electives which would satisfy a particular requirement. In many schools where there are larger student bodies, the development of a variety of courses from different disciplinary approaches should be encouraged.

2. *Colleges and universities should be encouraged to adopt ethics courses specifically designed for their various undergraduate programs.* These programs should inform students about the issues which will face them in their professional life.[28]

3. *Colleges and universities should be encouraged to increase the number of symposia, lectureships, and similar programs which give specific attention to ethics and value issues.* These kinds of enrichment programs also allow the college or university to bring

---

[27] *See* Deborah L. Rhode, *Ethics by the Pervasive Method*, 42 J. Legal Educ. 31, 34–35 (1992) (many law students have had no formal ethics training before coming to law school).

[28] As noted above, these programs would not only benefit other professions and societal interest generally, but would also advance the students' ability to deal with ethical and professional responsibility issues in law school. Our interest is significant but not selfish. *See generally,* Patricia M. King & Karen Strohm Kitchener, DEVELOPING REFLECTIVE JUDGMENT 230–57 (1994) (suggestions for fostering the development of reflective thinking in college undergraduate programs).

persons to the campus who have differing viewpoints on particular issues.

B. Law School Professionalism Training

Law school is where most law students first come into contact with issues relating to legal professionalism. Their law school experience has a profound influence on their professional values and their understanding of the practice of law and the role of lawyers in our society.

For most students law school professors are their first and most important role models of lawyers. Professionalism ideals can either be enhanced or undermined by the behavior of faculty in and out of the classroom. In a recent article, Professor Carrie Menkel-Meadow of UCLA Law School paints a rather grim picture of many current law faculty:

> If we examine our teaching rather than our more idealized scholarship, the real messages we convey about lawyering become more apparent—and less flattering. As others have noted, the traditional classroom fosters adversariness, argumentativeness, and zealotry, along with the view that lawyers are only the means through which clients accomplish their ends—what is "right" is whatever works for this particular client or this particular case. We extol loyalty to the client above moral and other concerns. Our case-by-case method, which focuses on identifying principles of doctrine rather than principles of behavior, also encourages moral relativism. The values that we attend to in the classroom are apt to be individualism and autonomy, which we present as the basis for the adversary system, the Bill of Rights, and the standard of proof in criminal cases. We fail to teach our students that lawyering involves responsibility to and for others. We may add new images to the traditional image of the lawyer as zealous advocate. But when we portray the contemporary lawyer as, for instance, a facilitator of market transactions in modern advanced capitalism, we usually fail to consider what it would mean to be more than a cog in the wheel of economic progress. We may be aware that we convey some of these messages; perhaps we are less aware of images of lawyering that our classroom interactions with students create. Most of us, for instance, communicate disdain for real world activity and practice. We undermine any authority we might have as purveyors of ethical messages about good lawyering when we suggest that law professors are the priests and lawyers the pimps or prostitutes of the profession. As we count out publications and *bon mots*, are we any better? Are we not committed to a sort of intellectual materialism? That is, are we not as interested as "real

world" lawyers are in maximizing income, if not in dollars, than in other tokens of fame? We may also appear to our students to care more about ideas than people. Getting the ideas or concepts "right" seems to matter more than the student's emotional health. Thus, our students are apt to become skeptical or cynical. Students, because they are laughed at, abandon the common sense and morality they bring to law school and may not relearn them after mastering the technicalities of law.[29]

To counteract this type of criticism, law schools must be more willing than in the past to hire as faculty lawyers who have extensive practice experience and to include public service by faculty positively in the faculty evaluation process.

Moreover, as a general rule, law schools have treated professionalism issues as being part of legal ethics, to be covered in whatever course or courses deal explicitly with that subject. Although there has been a great deal written about the pervasive method of teaching legal ethics throughout the entire curriculum,[30] law schools have, for the most part, merely given lip service to this approach.[31] Thus, the basic course in legal ethics or professional responsibility has become, by design or by lack of time, the main, if not the only, place in the law school curriculum where students are exposed in a systematic manner to professionalism issues.

Not only is the basic legal ethics course supposed to expose law students to the ethical rules that will govern them when they become practitioners, it is also supposed to provide them with information about the nature of the practice of law, the role of lawyers in our society, and to develop their capacity for reflective judgment.[32] It is virtually impossible to achieve all of these goals in a single, one-semester course. In fact, the available evidence indi-

---

[29] Carrie Menkel-Meadow, *Can a Law Teacher Avoid Teaching Legal Ethics?* 41 J. Legal Educ. 3, 6–8 (1991). *See also* Richard C. Baldwin, *Rethinking Professionalism—and Then Living It!* 41 Emory L. J. 433, 444–45 (1992) (importance of a law professor as a role model of lawyering).

[30] *See, e.g.,* James E. Starrs, *Crossing a Pedagogical Hellesport via the Pervasive System,* 17 J. Legal Educ. 365 (1965); E. Wayne Thode & T. A. Smedley, *An Evaluation of the Pervasive Approach to Education for the Professional Responsibility of Lawyers,* 41 U. Colo. L. Rev. 365 (1969). The arguments for and against the pervasive system are summarized in Ian Johnstone & Mary P. Treuthart, *Doing the Right Thing: An Overview of Teaching Professional Responsibility,* 41 J. Legal Educ. 75, 87–89 (1991).

[31] *See* Deborah L. Rhode, *supra* note 27, at 41 (author's survey of 138 books published by the three leading law school publishers in fourteen substantive areas, disclosed that the median coverage of ethics issues was 1.4 percent of the total pages in each volume); Michael J. Kelley, LEGAL ETHICS AND LEGAL EDUCATION 48–51 (1980).

[32] *See* Johnstone & Treuthart, *supra* note 30, at 42–43.

cates that despite good intentions to the contrary, coverage of the rules of professional conduct governing lawyers ends up being the main focus of the basic ethics course in most law schools.[33]

Providing additional classroom coverage of professionalism issues will not be an easy task. Law school curriculum reform is a tedious and often frustrating task[34] and seems to work best when modest changes are made at the margin by adding one or two additional courses.[35] If the proponents of the need for increased law school training in ethics and professionalism are right, however, an effort equivalent to that which led to the increase in clinical legal education in the 1970s and the increased emphasis on skills training in the 1990s is required. The aim of this effort should be to elevate the twin concepts of the practice of law as a public service calling and the development of the capacity for reflective moral judgment to the same level as legal knowledge and traditional legal skills. This is indeed an ambitious goal.

Some law schools, most notably Notre Dame, have already undertaken this task. Notre Dame Law School has implemented pervasive ethics coverage throughout the curriculum. Moreover, Notre Dame has three required ethics/professionalism courses.[36] The first-year course provides background material on ethical decision-making, exposes students to the important role of lawyers as independent counselors to their clients, and introduces students to the concept of justice.[37] The rules of professional conduct governing lawyers are only a small component of this course.[38] Notre Dame also has a required third-year applied ethics course and a perspective course requirement, which can be met by a number of different courses.[39]

---

[33] *See* William H. Simon, *The Trouble with Legal Ethics*, 41 J. Legal Educ. 65, 66 (1991); Johnstone & Treuthart, *supra* note 30, at 90–92.

[34] *See* John O. Mudd, *Academic Change in Law Schools: Part I*, 29 Gonz. L. Rev. 29 (1993/94); Part II, *Id.*, 225; *see also* Roger C. Cramton, *The Current State of the Law Curriculum*, 32 J. Legal Educ. 321 (1982).

[35] John C. Weistart, *The Law School Curriculum: The Process of Reform*, 1987 Duke L. J. 317, 322–23, 332–40. Several law schools have successfully implemented major curriculum reform proposals in recent years. *See, e.g.,* Curtis J. Berger, *A Pathway to Curricular Reform*, 39 J. Legal Educ. 547 (1989) (describes Columbia Law School's first-year changes); Gregory S. Muro, *Integrity Theory and Practice in a Competency-Based Curriculum: Academic Planning at the University of Montana School of Law*, 52 Mont. L. Rev. 345 (1991); Todd D. Rakoff, *The Harvard First-Year Experiment*, 39 J. Legal Educ. 491 (1989).

[36] *See* David T. Link, *The Pervasive Method of Teaching Ethics*, 39 J. Legal Educ. 485 (1989).

[37] *Id.* at 486–89.

[38] *Id.* at 486.

[39] *Id.* at 486.

This type of structural reform may not be possible to achieve in many law schools. Nevertheless, serious efforts to add professionalism components to the basic law school curriculum should be undertaken by all law schools.

To implement these suggestions, we recommend that law schools consider the following as part of a more effective program of teaching and learning professionalism. Most, if not all, of these suggestions are currently being implemented by various law schools. See Appendix B. No law school, however, has adopted all of these suggestions and it is not the intent of this Committee that a law school should implement all of them. Rather it is our intent that faculties consider all of them and adopt those that are best suited to their particular school.

1. *Faculty must become more acutely aware of their significance as role models for law students' perception of lawyering.*[40]

---

[40] *See, e.g.,* Stanley Commission Report, *supra* note 1, at 268–9; Richard C. Baldwin, *supra* note 29, at 444–45; Thomas D. Eisele, *Must Virtue Be Taught?* 39 J. Legal Educ. 495, 505–08 (1989).

The importance of law professors as role models is explicitly recognized in the *Statement of Good Practices by Law Professors in the Discharge of Their Ethical and Professional Responsibilities*, a voluntary aspirational statement adopted by the Executive Committee of the Association of American Law Schools in 1987. Examples include the following:

As teachers, scholars, counselors, mentors, and friends, law professors can profoundly influence students' attitudes concerning professional competence and responsibility. Professors should assist students to recognize the responsibility of lawyers to advance individual and social justice.

Because of their inevitable function as role models, professors should be guided by the most sensitive ethical and professional standards. . . .

Law professors have an obligation to treat students with civility and respect and to foster a stimulating and productive learning environment in which the pros and cons of debatable issues are fairly acknowledged.

• • •

One of the traditional obligations of members of the bar is to engage in uncompensated public service or pro bono legal activities. As role models for students and as members of the legal profession, law professors share this responsibility. This responsibility can be met in a variety of ways, including direct client contact through legal aid or public defender offices (whether or not through the law school), participating in the legal work of public-interest organizations, lecturing in continuing legal education programs, educating public school pupils or other groups concerning the legal system, advising local, state and national government officials on legal issues, engaging in legislative drafting, and/or other law reform activities.

The fact that a law professor's income does not depend on serving the interests of private clients permits a law professor to take positions on issues as to which practicing lawyers may be more inhibited. With that freedom from economic pressures goes an enhanced obligation to pursue individual and social justice.

Professors whose consulting or research activities make them unavailable for classes, regular office hours for consultations with students, or *pro bono* service send an unmistakable message to law students about these professors' and their law school's value system. Civility and human kindness toward students inside and outside the classroom are as important, if not more important, than a series of lectures on the precepts of litigation civility. Finally, criticism of practicing lawyers and the legal system by law school faculty should be constructive criticism designed to promote a better system of justice and good lawyering rather than, as is sometimes the case, a denigration of practicing lawyers and judges.[41]

2. *Greater emphasis needs to be given to the concept of law professors as role models of lawyering in hiring and evaluating faculty.* Teaching ethics and professionalism by example is not only effective from a learning perspective, but it is also cost-effective— no additional courses or resource allocations are required. Measures that law schools should consider in implementing a role model sensitivity policy include:

- Hiring as permanent, adjunct, and visiting faculty a significant number of experienced practitioners who have not only succeeded in the practice of law but also manifest a respect for and commitment to the legal profession and an understanding that part of their calling is to serve the public interest and to represent those who are disadvantaged by age or circumstance.
- Overcoming the apparent reluctance on the part of many faculties to hire lawyers with extensive practice experience as tenure track faculty.[42]

Ass'n of Amer. Law Schools, 1995 HANDBOOK 90, 94 (1995). The Florida Bar Commission on Lawyer Professionalism recommends that:
[l]aw schools should be encouraged to adopt the Statement and to abide by its aspirational goals, so that law faculty can provide in practice the proper role model for students, the Bar, and the public.
Florida Bar Commission on Professionalism, PROFESSIONALISM: A RECOMMITMENT OF THE BENCH, THE BAR, AND THE LAW SCHOOLS 19 (1989). How many law schools have formally adopted this Statement is unknown.

[41] *See* Jack L. Sammons, Jr., *Professing: Some Thoughts on Professionalism and Classroom Teaching*, 3 Geo. J. Legal Ethics, 609, 615–21 (1990); Menkel-Meadow *supra* note 29, at 6–9; Patrick Wiseman, *Legal Education and Cynicism About the Law: Practicing Ethical Jurisprudence in the Classroom*, 25 Cumb. L. Rev. 1 (1994).

[42] *See* Graham C. Lilly, *Law Schools Without Lawyers? Winds of Change in Legal Education*, 71 Va. L. Rev., 1421, 1457 (1995). The difference between academic and private sector compensation of lawyers rather than bias against practicing lawyers is, however, often the determining factor in the decision-making process for experienced lawyers who would like to become full-time law professors. Unless the economic conditions in higher education change, there is very little law schools can do to remedy this problem.

- Encouraging the use of successful, experienced lawyers and highly respected judges [43] as adjunct professors. Not only are they capable of teaching specialized and practice-oriented skills courses, they can also, by virtue of their experience and stature, serve as excellent role models for law students. In addition, they can give a real-world perspective to ethics and professionalism issues, because of their real-world experiences, and can readily integrate those issues into their courses.
- Assigning only faculty with extensive practice experience as well as a long-term commitment to the subject matter to teach the basic and advanced ethics and professionalism courses. It is very difficult for a law professor who has little or no practice experience to understand or to convey to students the context in which these issues arise and must be resolved.

3. *Adoption of the pervasive method of teaching legal ethics and professionalism should be seriously considered by every law school.* It is virtually impossible in a single two- or three-credit course to cover adequately all the ethical and professionalism issues that practicing lawyers and judges must identify and grapple with on a daily basis. These issues are inextricably involved in the practice of law and the pervasive method is the most effective way of inculcating this concept.[44] The goal of a successful pervasive method need not be that ethical and professionalism issues be covered in every law school course. A pervasive system should ensure that every law student is exposed to ethical and professionalism issues in a systematic fashion during each year of the J.D. program.[45] Without constant reinforcement, the training received in a basic ethics course becomes blunted over time and may be undermined by the experiences of law students who work as clerks in law firms

---

[43] *See, e.g.,* Il. S. Ct. Rules 64 (an Illinois judge cannot teach a class before 5:30 P.M.; must file a request for each course to be taught; and the supervising judge must certify that the proposed teaching will not interfere with the judge's judicial duties) and 66 (compensation from teaching cannot exceed $3,000 per six months).

[44] Chief Judge Harry T. Edwards of the District of Columbia Circuit Court of Appeals has expressed the need for the pervasive method in this fashion:

Law students need concrete ethical training. They need to know why *pro bono* work is so important. They need to understand their duties as "officers of the court." They need to learn that cases and statutes are normative texts, appropriately interpreted from a public-regarding point of view, and not mere missiles to be hurled at opposing counsel. They need to have great ethical teachers, and to have every teacher address ethical problems where such problems arise.

Harry T. Edwards, *The Growing Disjunction Between Legal Education and the Legal Profession*, 91 Mich. L. Rev., 34, 38 (1992).

[45] *See* the description of the Notre Dame Law School pervasive program described *supra* at notes 36–39 and accompanying text.

or who enroll in clinical or extern programs.[46] Each law school must design its own pervasive system based on its particular mission and available faculty and financial resources. Suggestions for implementing an effective pervasive system include:

- Elevating legal ethics and professionalism to the same level as the other major components of the curriculum. This will require treating this subject matter with the same seriousness and allocation of faculty and other resources as, for example, the business or commercial law curriculum. Under this perspective, the basic legal ethics course should be viewed as merely the first component of an overall ethics and professionalism program. At the very least, this basic course should explore the multi-dimensional aspects of the attorney-client relationship and the importance of the role of lawyers as counselors and problem-solvers as well as advocates of their clients' causes and introduce students to the aspirational concepts of professionalism; it should not be limited to merely covering the disciplinary rules with the view toward providing students with the knowledge necessary to pass the ethics component of the bar admission examination.[47] To accomplish these objectives, schools that currently have a two-credit-hour basic course should consider allocating three credit-hours to the course.[48]
- Providing a summer reading list on ethics and professionalism issues (e.g., *To Kill a Mockingbird*) to incoming law students.[49]

---

[46] *See* Lawrence K. Hellman, *The Effects of Law Office Work on the Formation of Law Students' Professional Values: Observation, Explanation, Optimization*, 4 Geo. J. Legal Ethics, 537 (1991) (describes widespread ethical violations observed by law students working as interns in law offices).

[47] *See* Gordon & Simon, *supra* note 17, at 235–36 ("The professional responsibility portions of bar examinations are exclusively concerned with testing knowledge of disciplinary rules. In part because of the influence of the bar exams, nearly all law school courses on professional responsibility focus on the rules, probably a majority exclusively so.").

[48] A 1985 survey of law school ethics courses showed that 75 percent of law schools that replied had a two-credit-hour course and 16 percent of the law schools had a three-credit-hour course. American Bar Ass'n Center for Professional Responsibility, A SURVEY ON THE TEACHING OF PROFESSIONAL RESPONSIBILITY 3 (1986). The 1994 law school survey conducted for this report showed that the percentage of law schools having a two-credit-hour basic course in legal ethics had declined to 44 percent and the percentage of law schools having a three-credit-hour course had increased to 23 percent. The remaining law schools had a two- or three-hour variable credit course or series of courses. *See* Appendix B.

[49] *See* Stanley Commission Report, *supra* note 1, at 267–68.

- Designing a course, or alternatively a lecture series, introducing first-year law students to important ethical and professionalism issues (one or more of the books on the summer reading list sent to incoming students might be discussed as part of this module).[50]
- The development of ethics and professionalism modules for all first-year substantive law courses and/or as part of a first-year lawyering skills course.[51]
- The development of ethics and professionalism modules for second- and third-year courses.[52] One possibility is to authorize an optional additional hour of credit for courses in which the students write a paper or produce another type of legal

---

[50] *See* the description of the Brigham Young University Law School Professional Seminar, the Valparaiso University first-year ethics course, and the Campbell College Law School professionalism lecture series in Exhibits 2, 3 and 4 of Appendix B. *See generally* Nancy M. Maurer & Linda F. Mischler, *Introduction to Lawyering: Teaching First Year Students to Think Like Professionals*, 44 J. Legal Educ. 96 (1994); Kent M. Saunders & Linda Levine, *Learning to Think Like a Lawyer*, 29 U.S.F. L. Rev. 121, 183–84 (1994).
Several texts suitable for an introductory course or lecture series on professionalism have recently been published. *See* Bailey Kuklin & Jeffrey W. Stempel, FOUNDATIONS OF THE LAW—AN INTERDISCIPLINARY AND JURISPRUDENTIAL PRIMER (1994); Michael G. Kelley, LIVES OF LAWYERS: JOURNEYS IN THE ORGANIZATIONS OF PRACTICE (1994); James E. Moliterno & Fredric Lederer, AN INTRODUCTION TO LAW, LAW STUDY AND THE LAWYER'S ROLE (1991); Thomas L. Shaffer & Robert F. Cochran, Jr., LAWYERS, CLIENTS AND MORAL RESPONSIBILITY (1994). There are also several perspective-oriented anthologies, containing readings and cases that can be used as the text or as supplemental materials for a course or series of lectures on legal ethics and professionalism. *See* Daniel R. Coquillette, LAWYERS AND FUNDAMENTAL MORAL RESPONSIBILITY (1995); Geoffrey C. Hazard, Jr. & Deborah L. Rhode, THE LEGAL PROFESSION: RESPONSIBILITY AND REGULATIONS (3rd ed. 1994); Philip B. Heymann & Lance Liebman, THE SOCIAL RESPONSIBILITIES OF LAWYERS: CASE STUDIES (1988); Howard Lesnick, BEING A LAWYER: INDIVIDUAL CHOICE AND RESPONSIBILITY IN THE PRACTICE OF LAW (1992); ETHICAL ISSUES IN PROFESSIONAL LIFE (Joan C. Callahan, ed. 1988); PROFESSIONAL RESPONSIBILITY ANTHOLOGY (Thomas B. Metzloff, ed. 1994).
[51] *See* the description of the Albany Law School Introduction to Lawyering course, *infra* Appendix B. *See also* Deborah L. Rhode, PROFESSIONAL RESPONSIBILITY—ETHICS BY THE PERVASIVE METHOD (1994) (contains material addressing ethical issues in the context of ten substantive areas including civil procedure, constitutional law, contracts, criminal law, property, and torts, all or most of which are included in the first-year curriculum of virtually every law school).
[52] *See* Rhode, *supra* note 51. In addition to the six substantive areas mentioned in note 51, this innovative paperback book also covers the principal ethical problems that arise in four other substantive law areas: corporations, evidence and trial advocacy, family law, and tax. *See also* David Luban & Michael M. Milleman. *Good Judgment: Ethics Teaching in Dark Times*, 9 Geo. J. Legal Ethics 31, 64–67 (1995) (description of a law school clinical course where students meet weekly to discuss ethical issues arising in their clinical work).

work product on one or more significant ethical or professionalism issues in the subject area of the course.[53]

- A requirement that ethical and professionalism issues be covered at a minimum in every skills-oriented course (e.g., interviewing, counseling and negotiation courses, pre-trial and
  trial practice courses, clinical courses and extern programs).
- The development of additional elective courses and seminars
  that focus on ethical and professionalism issues in the context
  of a particular substantive area of practice (e.g., The Professional Responsibility of the Litigator).[54]
- The development of additional perspective courses and seminars[55] that focus on multiculturalism and diversity, the inter-
  nationalization and globalization of law and law practice,[56]
  jurisprudence, legal history, and professionalism issues such
  as the strengths and weaknesses of our justice system, the
  role of lawyers in our society, and the sociology of lawyers
  and law firms.[57]
- A requirement that every student successfully complete at
  least one ethics and professionalism course or component
  each year.
- Developing an annual ethics and professionalism lecture
  series or symposium that is widely publicized within the law
  school community.

---

[53] This device could also be used to encourage innovative teaching techniques. *See infra* notes 65–67 and accompanying text. The professor teaching the course could, for example, use E-mail to communicate with those students who have chosen the extra-credit ethics professionalism module.

[54] Several law schools have developed these types of courses. *See infra* Appendix B.

[55] *See* Robert F. Drinin, *Perspective Courses and Co-Curricular Activities*, 41 U. Colo. L. Rev. 416 (1969); Lester J. Mazor & Donald B. King, *Perspective Courses and Co-Curricular Activities*, 41 U. Colo. L. Rev. 432 (1969). Course books suitable for these types of courses include: Anthony A. D'Amato & Arthur J. Jacobson, JUSTICE AND THE LEGAL SYSTEM (1992); Thomas L. Shaffer, AMERICAN LEGAL ETHICS: TEXT, READINGS AND DISCUSSION TOPICS (1985).

[56] *See* Deborah L. Rhode, *Institutionalizing Ethics*, 44 Case W. Res. L. Rev. 665, 733 (1994) ("More cross-professional, cross-cultural and cross-disciplinary material could help explore structural causes of ethical dilemmas and the merits of particular regulatory responses.").

[57] While some important pioneering work on the sociological behavior of lawyers has been conducted, much remains to be accomplished. *See, e.g.*, Jerome Carlin, LAWYERS ON THEIR OWN (1962); Marc Galanter & Thomas Paly, TOURNAMENT OF LAWYERS: THE GROWTH AND TRANSFORMATION OF THE LARGE LAW FIRM (1991); Ronald J. Gilson & Robert H. Mnookin, *Coming of Age in a Corporate Law Firm: The Economics of Associate Career Partners*, 41 Stan. L. Rev. 567 (1989); Carroll Seron, *Managing Entrepreneurial Legal Services: The Transformation of Small Firm Practice*, in LAWYER'S IDEALS/LAWYER'S PRACTICES, *supra* note 5, at 63; *Symposium: The Growth of Large Law Firms and Its Effect on the Legal Profession and Legal Education*, 64 Ind. L. J. 423 (1989).

- Encouraging the importance and open discussion of moral or reflective judgment in the classroom.[58] The once widely held view that ethical precepts are fully formed before law school has been proven to be untrue.[59] Judgment is an essential element of lawyering; and the failure to emphasize its importance in the classroom sends out the negative image that it is unimportant.[60]

- Emphasizing in the classroom and in other ways the concept of public service as a central tenet of lawyering. This involves an understanding of the relationship between lawyers' virtual monopoly over legal services, self-regulation and public service (which is the trade-off for the monopoly and self-regulation). In short, public service is not merely an aspiration or an ideology. It is the very essence of being a lawyer in our society.[61]

- Providing multiple opportunities for law students to express their concerns about the conflict between the requirements of legal ethics and their own personal values and to explore ways to resolve or at least reconcile those conflicts.[62] Reluctance or refusal to discuss these issues reinforces a cynical

---

[58] *See* Tom Clark, *Teaching Professional Ethics*, 12 San Diego L. Rev. 249 (1975); James R. Elkins, *The Pedagogy of Ethics*, 10 J. Legal Prof. 37 (1985); Gordon & Simon, *supra* note 17, at 236–37; Timothy L. Hall, *Moral Character, The Practice of Law and Legal Education*, 60 Miss. L. J. 511 (1990); Anthony T. Kronman, *Living in the Law*, 54 U. Chi. L. Rev. 835, 961–76 (1987); Banks McDowell, *The Usefulness of "Good Moral Character*,*"* 33 Wash. L. J. 323 (1994); John O. Mudd, *The Place of Perspective in Law and Legal Education*, 26 Gonz. L. Rev. 277 (1990/91); John V. Tunney, *Is the Bar Meeting Its Ethical Responsibility?* 12 San Diego L. Rev. 245 (1975).

[59] *See, e.g.*, Elliott M. Abramson, *Puncturing the Myth of the Moral Intractability of Law Students: The Suggestiveness of the Work of Psychologist Lawrence Kohlberg for Ethical Training in Legal Education*, 7 Notre Dame J. L. Ethics & Pub. Policy 223 (1993); Ronald M. Pipkin, *Law School Instruction in Professional Responsibility: A Curricular Paradox*, 1979 Amer. Bar Found. Res. J. 247, 265–75.

[60] *See, e.g.*, Rhode, *supra* note 27, at 50–51; Carrie Menkel-Meadow, *supra* note 29, at 3–4; Paul Brest & Linda Kreiger, *On Teaching Professional Judgment*, 69 Wash. L. Rev. 522 (1994). *But see* Lee Modjeska, *On Teaching Morality to Law Students*, 41 J. Legal Educ. 71 (1991) (the classroom should not be used as a bully pulpit for a professor's personal moral principles).

[61] *See, e.g.*, Stanley Commission Report, *supra* note 1, at 261–62, 265, 296–305; Luban, *supra* note 13, at 736–40; Terrell & Wildman, *supra* note 14, at 419–22, 428–32.

[62] *See, e.g.*, Terrance Sandalow, *The Moral Responsibility of Law Schools*, 34 J. Legal Educ. 163 (1984); Michael I. Swygert, *Striving to Make Great Lawyers—Citizenship and Moral Responsibility: A Jurisprudence for Law Teaching*, 30 Bos. Col. L. Rev. 803, 818–20 (1989). There are several recent publications suitable for use in law school courses exploring these issues. *See* Milner S. Ball, THE WORD AND THE LAW (1993); Morris Norval, THE BROTHEL BOY AND OTHER PARABLES OF THE LAW (1992); Thomas L. Shaffer, ON BEING A CHRISTIAN AND A LAWYER: LAW FOR THE INNOCENT (1981). *See also* the sources cited in note 50, *supra*.

attitude toward law and the practice of law that too often permeates law schools today.[63]

4. *Every law school should develop an effective system for encouraging and monitoring its ethics and professionalism programs.* Faculty development programs, faculty colloquia, faculty retreats, and even faculty meetings can be effective forums for discussion of these issues and presentations by faculty who, for example, have successfully integrated ethics and professionalism components into their courses. The dean's office or a faculty committee (for example the curriculum committee or the faculty development committee) should be given the responsibility for monitoring the pervasive system adopted by the law school. At the very least, the monitoring should include requiring course descriptions and course syllabi that describe or list the ethics and professionalism issues that are to be covered and annual discussions with faculty members participating in the pervasive program. Consideration should be given to one or more of the following:[64]

- Conducting a survey of existing courses to determine the extent to which ethical and professionalism issues are covered in the curriculum.[65]
- Appointing a faculty member as coordinator of the law school's ethics and professionalism programs.
- Joint preparation of syllabi by all faculty teaching courses having significant ethics or professionalism components.

---

[63] *See* Roger C. Cramton, *The Ordinary Religion of the Law School Classroom*, 29 J. Legal Educ. 247, 262–63(1978):

> Modern dogmas entangle legal education—a moral relativism tending toward nihilism, a pragmatism tending toward an amoral instrumentalism, a realism tending toward cynicism, an individualism tending toward atomism, and a faith in reason and democratic processes tending toward mere credulity and idolatry. We will neither understand nor transform these modern dogmas unless we abandon our unconcern for value premises. The beliefs and attitudes that anchor our lives must be examined and revealed.
>
> Our indifference to values confines legal education to the *"what is"* and neglects the promise of *"what might be."* It confirms a bias deeply ingrained in many law students—that law school is a training ground for technicians who want to function efficiently within the status quo.
>
> The aim of all education, even in a law school, is to encourage a process of continuous self-learning that involves the mind, spirit and body of the whole person. This cannot be done unless larger questions of truth and meaning are directly faced.

[64] A more complete list of suggestions that were made by various law schools in replying to the Law School Survey on Professionalism conducted by this Committee is contained in Appendix B.

[65] A recent survey at the University of Arkansas, Little Rock, identified 20 courses where legal ethics and professionalism issues are routinely raised. *See infra* Appendix B.

- Obtaining input and comments from students on the effectiveness of the professionalism components in the curriculum.
- A meeting before the beginning of each semester of all faculty teaching courses having a significant ethics or professionalism component to coordinate the coverage of these issues and to avoid gaps and unnecessary duplication.
- Including ethics and professionalism issues in substantive law examinations.
- Requiring faculty to report, on a semi-annual or annual basis, either formally or informally, the coverage of ethics and professionalism issues in their courses.
- The development of course-specific teaching materials (e.g., the ethical problems of criminal law) that can be easily integrated into existing substantive law courses.[66]

5. *The use of diverse teaching methods such as role playing, problems and case studies, small groups and seminars, story-telling and interactive videos to teach ethics and professionalism, should be encouraged.*[67] These teaching methods, which are widely used in other fields, provide more effective opportunities than the traditional Socratic method for law students to develop and nurture their capacity for reflective moral judgment and to express their concerns about our legal system and the conflict between the requirements of legal ethics and their own personal values.[68] Moreover, acquiring the growing number of videos on legal ethics and professionalism issues should be a high priority for law school libraries.[69] A current catalogue, together with explanatory material on the content of these materials, should be distributed to the faculty on a regular basis.

6. *Law book publishers should consider adopting a policy requiring that all new casebooks and instructional materials incorporate ethical and professionalism issues. Law book publishers should also publish more course-specific materials on legal ethics and professionalism issues as part of new casebooks, new*

---

[66] *See* Rhode, *supra* note 51 (addresses ethical issues in the context of ten substantive areas).

[67] *See, e.g.*, Johnstone & Treuthart, *supra* note 30, at 98–102; Carrie Menkel-Meadow, *Is Altruism Possible in Lawyering?*, 8 Ga. St. U. L. Rev. 385, 416–19. *See generally*, *Symposium, Lawyers as Storytellers & Storytellers as Lawyers*, 18 Vt. L. Rev. 67 (1994).

[68] *See* Gordon & Simon, *supra* note 17, at 240; Pipkin *supra* note 59, at 272–75.

[69] There are now several provocative videos containing vignettes that raise significant legal ethical issues. *See* Part B of Appendix G, *infra*, for a list of some of these videos.

editions of old casebooks, supplements to casebooks, compilations of supplemental readings, and compendiums.[70]

7. *Law schools need to develop more fully co-curricular activities, policies, and infrastructures that reflect a genuine concern with professionalism.*[71] The values reflected in the institutional framework of a law school have an important impact on law students' perception of what is important in the legal system. In addition to guest lectures and symposia on professionalism, law schools should consider establishing voluntary or mandatory *pro bono* and public service programs for students,[72] mentoring or other counseling and advisement programs, and inns of court.[73]

Moreover, law schools must provide an effective institutional framework for dealing with serious societal, ethical, and moral issues that arise in a law school setting including diversity, racial and gender discrimination, homophobia, sexual harassment, and the special needs of various groups of students such as disabled and non-traditional students.[74]

C. Teaching and Learning Professionalism in the Practice of Law

Law school can provide the framework for understanding and internalizing the unique American concept of legal professionalism and can sensitize law students to the important professionalism issues. The practice of law is where these concepts and ideals are put to the test of reality. Therefore, it is important to understand how professionalism is nurtured—or undermined—by law practice.

---

[70] *See, e.g.*, Rhode, *supra* note 51, which addresses ethical issues in the context of ten substantive law areas.

[71] *See* Michael Burns, *The Law School as a Model for Community*, 10 Nova L. J. 329 (1986). Gordon & Simon, *supra* note 17, at 240; Johnstone & Treuthart, *supra* note 30, at 96. *See also* Robert V. Stover, MAKING IT AND BREAKING IT—THE FATE OF PUBLIC INTEREST COMMITMENT DURING LAW SCHOOL 115–21 (1989).

[72] *See, e.g.*, James L. Baillie & Judith Bernstein-Baker, *In the Spirit of Public Service: Model Rule 6.1, The Profession and Legal Education*, 13 Law & Inequality 51 (1994); Jill Claifetz, *The Value of Public Service: A Model for Instilling a Pro Bono Ethic in Law School*, 45 Stan. L. Rev. 1695 (1993); Henry Rose, *Law Schools Should Be About Justice Too*, 40 Clev. St. L. Rev. 443, 448–50 (1992). *See also* William B. Powers, *Report on Law School Pro Bono Activities*, Syllabus 10 (Winter, 1995) (59 percent of law schools had either a voluntary or required *pro bono* program as of December 1993).

[73] *See* Joryn Jenkins. *The American Inns of Court: Preparing Our Students for Ethical Practice?*, 27 Akron L. Rev. 175 (1993).

[74] *See* MacCrate Commission Report, *supra* note 2, at 216–17.

As a general rule, the existing professionalism reports issued by bar associations discuss professionalism in terms of two categories of issues. The first is competency and quality of practice issues, for example, mandatory continuing legal education, skills training for newly admitted lawyers, lawyer quality-of-life issues, law firm quality-control measures, more effective sanctions for serious ethical violations, and restrictions on false advertising. The second category is justice system issues, for example, the necessity for more *pro bono* legal work by lawyers, civility codes to counter the excesses of the present adversarial system, and law reform activities, such as increased use of alternative dispute resolution devices and procedures which reduce the cost and delay of litigation. In the often-cited 1986 Stanley Commission Report by the American Bar Association Commission on Professionalism, for example, the recommendations were roughly equally divided between these two categories.[75]

While these programs for increasing professionalism are beneficial and should be encouraged, they, for the most part, lack a coherent underlying philosophy that is necessary to provide a dynamic framework for transforming law firms and the delivery of legal services.[76] As a consequence, these professionalism reports sometimes make recommendations that if implemented merely paper over symptoms but fail to address the deeper causes of the concerns raised about the decrease in professionalism.[77] Moreover, many of the recommendations are based on a nostalgic vision of a lawyer who can practice "in the spirit of public service" with little concern for economic considerations, a paradigm that has probably never existed; and others are designed merely to improve the public image of lawyers rather than challenging lawyers' self-image and their roles in our society.[78]

A viable teleology of applied professionalism must be grounded in reality. However much we might wish otherwise, practicing lawyers must devote significant amounts of their time to earning a living from their practice. Recent pervasive economic changes and the emphasis on income generated by rainmaking and billable hours

---

[75] *See* Stanley Commission Report, *supra* note 2, at 263–65.

[76] *See, e.g.,* Gillers, *supra* note 17; Terrell & Wildman, *supra* note 14, at 403–22.

[77] *See, e.g.,* Mashburn, *supra* note 16; Schneyer, *supra* note 16, at 372–90.

[78] *See* Mashburn, *supra* note 16, at 661–80; Thomas L. Shaffer, *Inaugural Howard Lichtenstein Lecture in Legal Ethics: Lawyer Professionalism as a Moral Argument*, 26 Gonz. L. Rev. 393, 398–405 (1990/91).

have increased the competitive pressures on lawyers;[79] and the present economic climate is likely to continue indefinitely. Thus, it is now more difficult, but, hopefully, not impossible, for practicing lawyers to achieve their professionalism goals.

In essence, legal professionalism represents the shared values and expectations of lawyers.[80] These values and expectations are basically transmitted through the communities in which lawyers live and work.[81] The principal "communities" in which lawyers operate as attorneys are: (1) law firms and other practice settings such as in-house counsel and lawyers who work for government agencies, (2) their relationships with clients, (3) interaction with other lawyers, judges, and public officials as a result of client representation, and (4) bar associations and related legal organizations. One of the main goals of professionalism programs should be to nurture and increase professionalism in all four of these communities.

The Committee submits the following recommendations for consideration by bar associations, lawyers, law firms, judges, and public officials who regulate lawyers:

1. *National, state, local, and speciality bar associations must assume a leadership role in defining and promoting professionalism ideals and in implementing professionalism programs that reach all their members.* Since the mid-1980s a significant number

---

[79] *See, e.g.*, Robert L. Nelson, *Ideology, Practice, and Professional Autonomy: Social Values and Client Relationships in the Large Law Firm*, 37 Stan. L. Rev. 503, 506–09 (1985). *See also* Deborah L. Rhodes & David Luban, LEGAL ETHICS 43 (2nd ed. 1995) ("The lawyer-statesman is losing ground to the lawyer-entrepreneur. In many professional contexts, what is consistently regarded is less character and craft than rainmaking and billable hours.").

[80] Admittedly, not every lawyer agrees with every value or aspiration discussed in this report and in the vast literature on professionalism issues. Nevertheless, lawyers in the country have, in the main, historically subscribed to a common core of values and traditions, which we have tried to encapsulate in our definition of professionalism in Part I(C). The apparent loss of this broad consensus in recent years is the principal focus in much of the recent literature decrying the decline of professionalism in the United States. See the sources cited in notes 5–7, *supra*. The purpose of this report is to suggest ways which will reinvigorate and instill a shared consensus among contemporary lawyers. Whether this new consensus will be the same as or different from the historical consensus is a legitimate and important issue for discussion and debate which should take place in a climate that encourages and nurtures a dynamic dialogue of all points of view.

[81] *See* Terrell & Wildman, *supra* note 14, at 422; Jack L. Sammons, J. & Linda H. Edwards, *Honoring the Law in Communities of Force: Terrell and Wildman's Teleology of Practice*, 41 Emory L. J. 489, 504–11 (1992). *See also* Rhode, *supra* note 56, at 729 ("In many ways, the most elusive but also the most important strategy for institutionalizing professional ethics involves professional socialization. . . . [A]s practitioners themselves generally acknowledge, the most important influence in resolving ethical issues, apart from general upbringing, is professional environment.").

of bar associations have established professionalism committees that have produced reports containing multiple recommendations for revitalizing and nurturing professionalism. In far too many cases, however, these recommendations have not been implemented or have only been partially implemented. The most prominent work products of these committees to date have been aspirational civility and professionalism codes and creeds.[82] These are important first steps in a comprehensive professionalism program and all courts and bar associations should consider adopting these types of codes. Additional steps that should be seriously considered include the following:

- Holding a statewide series of meetings between lawyers, judges, and public officials designed to heighten the sensitivity to the decline of professionalism among lawyers and to galvanize support for a comprehensive professionalism program.[83]

- Having a voluntary or mandatory one- or two-day program for newly admitted lawyers that is presented just before they are sworn in, or at the latest within a year after their admission to practice, covering a wide range of professionalism issues including practical ethics, court room etiquette and civility, codes of professionalism, lists of available *pro bono* activities, and a review of available mentoring programs and other lawyer assistance programs.[84] This program could be included as part of an existing Bridge-the-Gap program or as a separate program that is presented in several locations across the state.

- Encouraging the inclusion of relevant ethics and professionalism issues in, and developing suitable course materials for, all CLE courses and Bridge-the-Gap programs.[85]

---

[82] *See infra* Appendix C.

[83] *Id.*

[84] At least three states (Arizona, Maryland, and Virginia) already have such a program. *See Id. See also* NEW YORK COURT OF APPEALS COMMITTEE ON THE PROFESSION AND THE COURTS, FINAL REPORT TO THE CHIEF JUDGE 24–25 (1995) (lists eight states having mandatory skills training programs for newly admitted lawyers, including an innovative three-year program in New Jersey). Recommendations advocating a formal internship or apprenticeship as a prerequisite to a full license to practice law have also recently been made by bar association committees. *See Id.* at 24–25. American Bar Ass'n, JUST SOLUTIONS—SEEKING INNOVATION AND CHANGE IN THE AMERICAN JUSTICE SYSTEM 60 (1994); *Florida Bar Commission on Lawyer Professionalism, supra* note 40 at 19. *See also* Alan S. Nemeth, *Taking Care of the Middle Class*, 80 A.B.A.J. 72 (Sept. 1994).

[85] Some CLE providers, e.g., ALI-ABA, currently have this requirement as part of their program procedures.

- Instituting a minimum ethics and professionalism hour requirement as part of a mandatory CLE program,[86] granting mandatory CLE hours credit for these programs, and developing suitable course materials, including interactive videos, for ethics and professionalism programs.[87]
- Establishing a voluntary special certification program for lawyers and law firms that meet rigorous ethical standards and procedures, including financial controls (e.g., trust account standards, audited financial statements), a sophisticated conflicts-of-interest check system, risk management procedures (e.g., "two-partner" rule for legal opinions, procedures for monitoring billing practices and outside activities of the lawyers in the firm that might create serious conflict-of-interest or malpractice issues), client relation procedures (e.g., an effective procedure for dealing with client complaints when they first arise), continuing legal education requirements, participation in *pro bono* activities, strict standards for legal advertising and other public relations activities, and peer review of the firm's legal work.[88]
- Establishing a mentor program under which experienced lawyers mentor newly admitted lawyers.[89]
- Establishing a lawyer resource directory containing the names of local lawyers in a speciality area who volunteer,

---

[86] Approximately 20 states already have a mandatory ethics/professionalism requirement. *See* MacCrate Commission Report, *supra* note 2, at 312.

[87] *See* Part B of Appendix G *infra* for a list of existing ethics/professionalism videos.

[88] *See* Geoffrey C. Hazard, Jr., *Certification Can Boost Right Control*, Nat'l L. J. at A21(August 29, 1994). *See also* John C. Buchaman, *The Demise of Legal Professionalism: Accepting Responsibility and Implementing Change*, 28 Val. U. C. Rev. 563, 576–81 (1994) (proposes a limited membership society of lawyers who are committed to the best ideals of professionalism, including community service). *See generally* ALI-ABA, LAW PRACTICE QUALITY EVALUATION: AN APPRAISAL OF PEER REVIEW AND OTHER MEASURES TO ENHANCE PROFESSIONAL PERFORMANCE (1988); *Id.*, THE QUALITY PURSUIT: ASSURING STANDARDS IN THE PRACTICE OF LAW (Robert M. Greene, ed. 1989); Susan R. Martyn, *Peer Review and Quality Assurance for Lawyers*, 20 U. Tol. L. Rev. 245 (1989).

[89] *See* Linda McDonald, *Legal Education and the Practicing Bar: A Partnership of Reality* in the MACCRATE REPORT—BUILDING THE EDUCATIONAL CONTINUUM, 105 (1993) (describes the New Mexico mentor system for recently admitted lawyers; both the mentors and the mentees receive mandatory CLE credit for their participation). The Minnesota State Bar Association has a mentor program called "Colleague" under which experienced lawyers volunteer to answer questions from other lawyers in one of 25 areas of law. The program has been operational since 1988. *See Colleague Program Serves Lawyers at Both Ends of the Line*, 9 MSBA In Brief 1 (Sept. 1993). In addition, the MSBA Board of Governors recently adopted comprehensive guidelines for an intra-law firm mentor system. A copy of these guidelines is reproduced in Appendix E.

assuming there is no conflict, to answer basic questions that less experienced lawyers may have in that subject area.[90]

- Sponsoring regular bench/bar conferences which have as one of their primary purposes the airing of etiquette, civility, and professionalism issues in the particular district or circuit.
- Increasing the number of *pro bono* and reduced-fee opportunities available for practicing lawyers [91] and coordinating and facilitating these activities and programs.[92]
- Establishing one or more local inns of court as part of the American Inns of Court program.[93]
- Sponsoring in-house training and CLE programs that are designed to sensitize all lawyers to the need to eliminate the vestiges of sexual harassment and gender, sexual orientation, and racial discrimination in law firms and the judicial system.[94]
- Implementing a lawyer quality of life program designed to make law firm working conditions more compatible with the professional as well as the personal goals of lawyers. One example is a recommendation that time devoted to *pro bono* activities should count toward a law firm's minimum billable hour requirement and also that such work should be taken

---

[90] *See, e.g.*, AMERICAN BAR ASS'N LAW PRACTICE MANAGEMENT SECTION 1994–95 MENTORING PROGRAM DIRECTORY (1994).

[91] *See* Model Rule 6.1 (sets an aspirational goal of 50 hours of *pro bono* work per year for every lawyer). MacCrate Commission Report, *supra* note 2, at 214–15 (providing *pro bono* service is an essential element of striving to promote justice, fairness and morality, one of the four fundamental values of the legal profession). *See also* Debra Burke, Regan McLaurin & James W. Pearle, *Pro Bono Publico: Issues and Implications*, 26 Loy. U. Chi. L.J. 61 (1994) (empirical study of large law firm *pro bono* activities). There is continuing debate as to whether the *pro bono* obligation extends only to the very poor, should be mandatory or merely voluntary, is the personal obligation of every lawyer or can be delegated to other lawyers in the firm or in the community, or should be financed in whole or in part by a special tax on lawyers' income. *See, e.g.*, Tigram W. Eldred & Thomas Schoenherr, *The Lawyer's Duty of Public Service: More Than Charity*, 96 W. Va. L. Rev. 367 (1994) (mandatory obligation); Marvin E. Frankel, *Proposed: A National Legal Service*, 45 S.C. L. Rev. 887 (1994) (proposes a publicly financed national judicare system); B. George Ballman, Jr., *Amended Rule 6.1: Another Move Towards Mandatory Pro Bono? Is That What We Want?*, 7 Geo. J. Legal Ethics 1139 (1994) (opposes a mandatory rule).

[92] One of the most interesting and innovative programs along this line is the American Bar Association Law Firm Pro Bono Challenge project, which is aimed at the 500 largest law firms in the country. Each signatory is required to make a commitment to contribute either three or five percent of the firm's total billable hours to *pro bono* work. Started in 1993, 169 firms had signed up for this program by the end of June 1995. The Statement of Principles and the Commentary to the Statement of Principles are reproduced in Appendix D.

[93] *See* FINAL REPORT OF THE COMMITTEE ON CIVILITY OF THE SEVENTH FEDERAL CIRCUIT 10 (1992).

[94] Several of the video programs listed in Part B of Appendix G are specifically designed for this purpose.

into account in a positive light in determining whether a lawyer should be made a partner in the firm.[95]

- Sponsoring a conclave of lawyers, judges, and legal academics to discuss the appropriate roles of each in legal education and including as an integral part of the conclave the teaching of ethics and professionalism on a continuum basis.[96]

2. *Practicing lawyers must become more acutely aware of the need to nurture and to renew their professionalism ideas on a continuing basis, always aspiring to maintain the highest standards of the lawyer-statesman paradigm.* Lawyers should be willing to share their knowledge and experience through mentoring and teaching other lawyers by participating in informal and formal mentoring programs and continuing legal education programs; and they should welcome the opportunity to participate in *pro bono* programs, non-partisan law reform activities[97] and other programs that promote and enhance professionalism among lawyers. Practicing lawyers also need to do a better job of developing in themselves and in their law firms a client-centered mentality where the expectations and objectives of clients and the human relations aspects of the lawyer-client relationship, rather than the potential legal fees in a particular matter, are the principal focus.[98]

3. *Law firms should adopt standards of practice and risk management procedures that enhance the level of competence and effi-*

---

[95] *See generally* BREAKING TRADITIONS—WORK ALTERNATIVES FOR LAWYERS (Donna M. Killougey, ed. 1994); Aimee McKim, *Comment, the Lawyer Track: The Case for Humanizing the Career Within a Large Firm*, 55 Ohio St. L. J. 176 (1994); Judith L. Maute, *Balanced Lives in a Stressful Profession: An Impossible Dream?* 21 Cap. U. L. Rev. 797 (1992); Carrie Menkel-Meadow, *Culture Clash in the Quality of Life in the Law: Changes in the Economic, Diversification and Organization of Lawyering*, 44 Case W. Res. L. Rev. 621, 656–62 (1994) (advocates greater experimentation and flexibility in law office work organization and compensation arrangements).

[96] Several states, including Virginia, North Carolina, Ohio, Illinois, and Louisiana have recently held conclaves. *See* AMERICAN BAR ASS'N COORDINATING COMMITTEE ON LEGAL EDUCATION, STATE BAR AND LEGAL EDUCATION CONCLAVES (1994).

[97] *See* Gordon & Simon, *supra* note 17, at 256 ("In such settings . . . [lawyers] may to some extent escape both the parochialism of their usual associates and the narrow advocacy roles and be free to articulate more disinterested views of ethics and policy.").

[98] *See* Robert M. Bastros, *Client Centered Counseling and Moral Accountability for Lawyers*, 10 J. Legal Prof. 97 (1985); Demetrious Dimitriou, *The Individual Practitioner and Commercialism in the Profession: How Can the Individual Survive?* 45 S.C.L. Rev. 965 (1994); Harry J. Haynsworth IV, *Alternatives to Value Billing: A Response to Demetrious Dimitriou, Id.* at 981; Carrie Menkel-Meadow, *Narrowing the Gap by Narrowing the Field: What's Missing from the MacCrate Report—Of Skills, Legal Science and Being a Human Being*, 69 Wash. L. Rev. 393 (1994). *See generally*, Bachman, *supra* note 10.

ciency of all the lawyers in their law firm.[99] In-house training programs for associates should include a review of these standards and procedures and the firm's expectations for the ethical standards and professionalism ideals of its lawyers. Ethics and professionalism issues should be included in the agenda for every law firm retreat.[100]

4. *Practicing lawyers need to become more sensitive to important quality of life issues and implement in their law firms enlightened working conditions that are compatible with the personal as well as the professional goals of the firm's lawyers.*[101] In particular, the ethical and other problems created by excessive billable hour and income requirements should be more openly acknowledged and remedied. As one highly regarded commentator recently stated:

> At an increasing number of firms, annual billable hour requirements exceed 2000 hours, and the additional work required to generate billable time makes for unduly demanding schedules. Experts generally agree that the hourly minimums at many law firms are unattainable without making "very liberal allowances" for the way in which time is recorded. Similar allowances are often made in assessing clients' "needs" and staffing their cases. Policing through normal market mechanisms is not always effective because consumers lack information about how best to achieve certain objectives, how much time a given task usually requires, how much time their attorney actually spends, and how cost effective the services are.

> Among bar leaders, most responses to these problems appear obvious but unpalatable. One strategy is to reduce annual billing requirements to levels that do not invite meter running or padding. Although this suggestion is typically dismissed as financially unrealistic if not ruinous, it bears note who is doing the dismissing. The partners who benefit from 2000 hour demands generally earn many times the national average for lawyers. If these partners' incomes were halved, they would still remain among the nation's highest earners. Those who would benefit from more humane expectations of billable hours constitute a much broader group. It includes attorneys who are reluctant to fudge, yet who cannot honestly fulfill current requirements without compromising family, pro bono, or other commitments. Conventional wisdom just a few decades ago was that lawyers could not reasonably expect to charge for more than 1200 to 1500 hours per year.

---

[99] After all, the delivery of quality legal services to clients at a fair price is a public service of the highest order. *See* Sammons, *supra* note 41, at 612–20.

[100] In-house law firm training programs have proliferated in recent years. *See* MacCrate Commission Report, *supra* note 2, at 314–16.

[101] *See* the sources cited in note 95, *supra*.

What has not changed is the number of hours in a day. Additional beneficiaries of more realistic billing requirements would be clients who want to minimize unnecessary or unproductive services by beleaguered attorneys blearily "going through the motions."[102]

5. *All law firms should have one or more committees that monitor the firm's compliance with ethical rules, continuing legal education requirements, risk management procedures, pro bono activities, quality of life, and other professionalism issues.* Associates should serve on these committees and all attorneys and the staff in a law firm should be encouraged to submit issues to these committees. Sole practitioners and small law firms should use lawyers in other firms to perform these review and oversight functions.

6. *Judges and judicial organizations must take a greater leadership role in raising the level of professionalism among practicing lawyers.* Consideration should be given to one or more of the following suggestions:

- Adopting civility codes and rules of etiquette applicable in their courts.[103]
- Requiring high levels of preparation and making it clear that failure to adequately prepare for a motion or trial will not be tolerated.
- Adopting court rules and procedures which reduce the cost and delay of litigation and encourage the use of alternative dispute resolution devices.[104]
- Sponsoring and participating in bench/bar conferences where current issues of civility, etiquette, and professionalism can be openly discussed.[105]
- Being willing to report to the appropriate disciplinary authority instances of incompetence and lack of professionalism that violate ethical rules.

---

[102] Rhode, *supra* note 56, at 710–11. *See also* Bachman, *supra* note 10, at 100–11, 137–40.

[103] *See infra* Appendix C. *See generally* Marvin E. Aspin, *The Search for Renewed Civility in Litigation*, 28 Val. U. L. Rev. 513 (1994).

[104] *See* 28 U.S. C §§101–471, 82 Pub. L. 101–650 (1990); Joseph R. Biden, Jr., *Equal Accessible, Affordable Justice Under Law: The Civil Justice Reform Act of 1990*, 1 Cornell L. J. & Publ. Policy 1 (1992); Jeffrey J. Peck, *"Users United": The Civil Justice Reform Act of 1990*, 54 Law & Contemp. Probs. 105 (1991).

[105] Judges should also be willing to point out etiquette, ethics, and professionalism issues to lawyers practicing in their courts on an informal, private basis.

- Volunteering to teach courses and to present lectures in law schools and continuing legal education programs on ethics and professionalism issues.[106]
- Adopting modern disciplinary procedures that effectively and efficiently result in appropriate sanctions for serious ethical violations.[107]
- Adopting programs like The Lawyers Ethics School[108] and Lawyer Assistance Programs that have as their primary goal rehabilitation and prevention of more serious ethical and professionalism problems.[109]

---

[106] *But see* Il. Ct. Rules 64 and 66 (prohibits Illinois state judges from teaching before 5:30 P.M. and imposes a maximum limit of $6,000 per year as compensation for teaching and other non-judicial activities).

[107] *See* American Bar Ass'n, REPORT OF THE COMMISSION ON EVALUATION OF DISCIPLINARY ENFORCEMENT (1991).

[108] *See The Florida Bar Plans to Establish an Ethics School*, Bar Leader 29 (July/Aug. 1992) (article points out that at least two other states, California and Virginia, have similar ethics schools for practicing lawyers who have had grievances filed against them that are found not serious enough to justify a disciplinary sanction).

[109] *See* American Bar Ass'n Comm'n on Impaired Attorneys, AN OVERVIEW OF LAWYER ASSISTANCE PROGRAMS IN THE UNITED STATES (1991). New York Court of Appeals Committee on the Profession and the Courts, *supra* note 84, at 47–48. *See generally*, Manual R. Ramos, *Legal Malpractice: The Profession's Dirty Little Secret*, 47 Vand. L. Rev. 1657, 1698–99 (1994).

III. Conclusion

Increasing the level of professionalism in American lawyers will not be an easy task. Fundamental changes in the education and socialization of lawyers and in the way law is currently practiced will be necessary. This process will take considerable time and will require a great deal of willpower and discipline by all of us, individually and collectively.

While the Committee's recommendations are phrased in terms of a series of specific suggestions and alternatives rather than mandates, the members of the Committee are convinced that selecting and implementing only a few of the suggestions in each area will not create the proper atmosphere to nurture a renewed sense of shared values that are a necessary precondition for professionalism to flourish. It is time to move beyond mere rhetoric and to galvanize ourselves for the challenge of moving ahead. The future of the American legal profession as a true profession hangs in the balance.[110]

---

[110] Not everyone agrees that American lawyers will successfully meet this challenge. See the quote from Dean Anthony T. Kronman, *The Lost Lawyer: Failing Ideals in the Legal Profession, supra*, at page 9. Another pessimistic view is that of Robert L. Nelson and David M. Trubek on page 14 of their introductory chapter entitled "New Problems and New Paradigms in Studies of the Legal Profession," *Lawyers' Ideals/Lawyers' Practices—Transformations in the American Legal Profession* (1992):

> The bar is too fragmented to agree on what relationships and values should be fostered. It has been too tolerant of entrepreneurship and too leery of effective professional association or governmental control to develop truly powerful regulatory mechanisms. The concerns of both the losers and at least some of the winners in the recent growth and restructuring of the industry made it important for bar leaders to say something comforting about professionalism and its value as an integrating element for the profession. The general sense that lawyers had lost control of their markets, workplaces, and careers has created a climate in which such rhetoric finds a ready audience. But a long tradition of entrepreneurship, segmentation, and weak control makes it impossible for the leaders of the bar to say or do anything significant about the trends they decry. The result is a vague and general invocation of "shared" values that really aren't shared and a symbolic and nostalgic crusade in the name of an ideology almost no one really believes in fully and which has little to do with the everyday working visions of American lawyers.

Appendix A

American Bar Association
Section of Legal Education and Admissions to the Bar

Professionalism Committee
1993–1996

Chairperson

Wm. Reece Smith, Jr., Esq.
Carlton, Fields, Ward, Emmanuel,
  Smith & Cutler, P.A.
One Harbour Place
777 South Harbour Island Drive
Tampa, FL 33602

Members

Honorable Dennis W. Archer
  (1993–94)
Mayor, City of Detroit
1126 City/County Building
Detroit, MI 48226

Martha W. Barnett, Esq. (1993–94)
Holland & Knight
315 South Calhoun Street, Suite 600
Post Office Drawer 810
Tallahassee, FL 32301

Dean Arthur Gaudio (1994–96)
University of Wyoming
College of Law
21st and Willett Drive
P. O. Box 3035
Laramie, WY 82071

Dean Harry Haynsworth
William Mitchell College of Law
875 Summit Avenue
St. Paul, MN 55105

Professor Emeritus
  Richard G. Huber (1993–94)
Boston College Law School
c/o Roger Williams University
  School of Law
Ten Meticom Avenue
Bristol, RI 02809-2921

Dean David T. Link
Notre Dame Law School
Notre Dame, IN 46556

Professor David Logan (1994–96)
Wake Forest University
School of Law
P. O. Box 7206
102 Carswell Hall, Gulley Drive
Winston–Salem, NC 27109

Dean Percy Luney
North Carolina Central University
School of Law
1512 South Alston Avenue
Durham, NC 27707

Rachael Martin (1995–96)
Executive Director
Texas Board of Law Examiners
P.O. Box 13486
Austin, TX 78711-3486

Judy Perry Martinez, Esq.
  (1994–96)
30th Floor Energy Building
1100 Poydras Street
New Orleans, LA 70163

Professor Michael K. McChrystal
  (1995–96)
Marquette University School of
  Law
Sensenbrenner Hall
1103 West Wisconsin Avenue
Milwaukee, WI 53201

Fred P. Parker III (1995–96)
Executive Director
Board of Bar Examiners of the
  State of North Carolina
208 Fayetteville Street
Raleigh, NC 27602

37

Chief Judge Randall T. Shepard
(1995–96)
Supreme Court of the State of
Indiana
304 State House
Indianapolis, IN 46204

Sharp Whitmore, Esq. (1993–95)
2005 Gird Road
Fallbrook, CA 92028

**Consultant on Legal Education
to the American Bar Association**
Professor James P. White
American Bar Association
Indiana University
550 West North Street
Indianapolis, IN 46202-3162

**Assistant Consultant to the
American Bar Association**
William B. Powers, Esq.
American Bar Association
Indiana University
550 West North Street
Indianapolis, IN 46202-3162

**American Bar Association
Staff Director**
Carol A. Weiss
American Bar Association
750 North Lake Shore Drive
Chicago, IL 60611

**American Bar Association
Assistant Staff Director**
Suzanne E. Rose
American Bar Association
750 North Lake Shore Drive
Chicago, IL 60611

Appendix B

Law School Survey on Professionalism

A. Introduction
B. Survey Results

A. *Introduction*

At the request of the Professionalism Committee, Bill Powers of the Section of Legal Education and Admissions to the Bar Staff distributed a questionnaire to all accredited law schools in June of 1994. The questionnaire was designed to determine the extent to which issues relating to professionalism are taught in law schools. There were essentially three questions. The first asked each school to list each course in the curriculum that deals with either legal ethics or professionalism, to state the credit hours for each of these courses and to describe whether they are required or elective and whether they are taught in the first or second or third year. The second question asked whether the law school taught ethics and professionalism on a pervasive basis throughout the curriculum, and if so, whether the pervasive system was mandatory or merely encouraged. An additional part of this question also asked how the school's pervasive system was implemented and monitored. The final question asked for a description of measures that "would be desirable to encourage the increased exposure of law students to legal ethics and professionalism issues."

Replies were received from 131 law schools or 74 percent of all accredited law schools. This is an excellent response rate. Representatives of all types of law schools in this country, large, medium, and small, public and private, urban and rural are included. Therefore, the data received from the questionnaire should present a fairly accurate overall picture of the extent to which ethics and professionalism issues are taught in American law schools at the present time. Because the questionnaire was deliberately made short in order to obtain a high response rate, however, the conclusions reached in this analysis of the results must be viewed as broad generalizations that might be subject to modification and refinement if more data from each law school had been received. The syllabi and course descriptions that accompanied the responses raised as many questions as they answered. The Professionalism Committee might want to consider a follow-up survey to a selected group of law schools, especially those who have innovative or unusual ethics and professionalism courses and programs.

B. Survey Results

The most common configuration is a single required two- (58 schools—44 percent of the total number responding) or three- (30 schools—23 percent of the total number responding) credit course entitled Legal Ethics or Professional Responsibility taught in the second or third year.* An additional six schools (5 percent of the total number responding) have a single course that has a variable credit hour allocation, typically 2–3 hours, depending apparently on who is teaching the course. Eight law schools (6 percent of the total number responding) require law students to take one of a series of courses. The University of North Carolina School of Law, for example, requires its students to take one of the following four courses in the second or third year:

Professional Responsibility (2)

Professional Responsibility of the Litigator (2)

Ethics in Criminal Practice (2)

Professionalism & Morality (3)

An additional twelve law schools (9 percent of the total responding) have a required upper-level course that is difficult to classify. They range from 1 credit hour (University of California–Davis) to 6 credit hours (Cornell, which has an innovative Lawyers and Clients course).

Nineteen law schools (14 percent of the total responding) require a legal ethics/professionalism credit component in the first year. Five offer a standard 2–4 credit-hour course. Eight have a one-hour first-year legal ethics/professionalism component. With one exception (Duke, which has a one-week intensive course that is taught between the first and second semesters), these schools all have an additional upper-level required ethics/professionalism course. Three law schools incorporate legal ethics and professionalism into their regular substantive law school courses (e.g., civil procedure at Drake). The remaining three (Albany, City College of New York, and William and Mary) have innovative first-year courses in which law students are exposed to ethical and professionalism issues in the context of an integrated skills training program in

---

* A 1985 law school survey conducted by the American Bar Association Center for Professional Responsibility found that 75 percent of respondents had a basic two-credit professional responsibility course and 16 percent had a basic three-credit professional responsibility course. *See* American Bar Ass'n Center for Professional Responsibility, A Survey on the Teaching of Professional Responsibility 3 (1986).

which the students are divided into law firms. The following description of the Albany Law School Introduction to Lawyering course is fairly typical of these types of programs:

> This course, an alternative to the traditional Legal Writing, Reasoning and Research course, combines legal writing with clinical methodology and professional skills development in order to teach students what lawyers do and how the legal system works. Students are assigned to one of two "law firms" and represent either a plaintiff or a defendant in a simulated lawsuit. During the year, they follow the hypothetical case through the legal process from initial client interview to appeal. In addition to completing research exercises and writing projects similar to those assigned in the traditional Legal Writing, Reasoning and Research course, students are introduced to practical skills including client counseling and interviewing, drafting of pleadings, discovery of facts, case planning, negotiating, and oral advocacy. Substantive and procedural law pertaining to the problem, and related problems of professional responsibility are also incorporated into the curriculum.

Finally, eight of the schools responding (6 percent of the total responses) have no required ethics or professionalism courses. One or more courses on these topics are, however, offered at each of these schools.

A majority of law schools listed more than one course which covers ethical and professionalism issues. A substantial number of schools (55 or 42 percent of those that responded), however, only listed one course dealing specifically with these issues. Many, if not most, of these law schools probably cover ethical issues in some other courses, but the person filling out the questionnaire apparently thought that only courses called legal ethics or the like were supposed to be listed. For example, the University of Arkansas–Little Rock reported that a recent faculty survey identified 20 courses where legal ethics and professionalism issues are routinely raised. Several other law schools listed clinics, interviewing, counseling, negotiations, evidence, trial practice, and even jurisprudence as courses where ethics and professionalism issues are covered.

The course descriptions in most of the courses titled legal ethics or professional responsibility listed professionalism or issues related to professionalism as part of the coverage. How much time is devoted to professionalism, as opposed to an analysis of the ethical rules governing lawyers, in these courses is impossible to determine. It is doubtful that a significant amount of time can be devoted to professionalism issues in a two-credit-hour course that is the basic required or elective legal ethics course.

Only sixteen law schools listed courses where professionalism is the principal focus. Some of these are courses or seminars with esoteric names (e.g., Psychodynamics of Lawyering—Rutgers [Newark]). The course description from two of these courses, the Professional Seminar from Brigham Young University and the first-year legal ethics course from Valparaiso, are attached as Exhibits 1 and 2. Other law schools undoubtedly offer credit courses having significant professionalism components, but it is difficult to determine these courses from the answers to the questionnaire.

Finally, seven law schools (University of Baltimore, Campbell University, Emory University, University of Georgia, Georgia State, St. Louis University, and Southern Illinois University) have one or more lectures on professionalism issues as part of an orientation program or a first-year non-credit course. Material on the Campbell University first-year professionalism lecture series is attached as Exhibit 3.

The three questions concerning the pervasive coverage of legal ethics and professionalism apparently proved to be somewhat confusing. Slightly over one-third of the law schools that responded (48) stated that their school had not adopted the pervasive method. Approximately two-thirds of the respondents stated that they had implemented a pervasive program. The vast majority of these schools indicated that the pervasive program was not mandatory. Rather it was merely encouraged by the dean and/or the faculty development or curriculum committee. Only sixteen law schools described a monitoring system for enforcing a mandatory pervasive program, although many additional law schools said they had a mandatory program. The monitoring systems reported included the following:

University of Baltimore—The faculty development committee holds programs on professionalism issues and the need to cover these issues in courses.

Brigham Young—Teachers of first-year courses are given a handout which lists professional responsibility issues applicable to their class and report at the end of the year to a faculty colleague who serves as coordinator.

Case Western—A faculty/student professionalism committee monitors progress of the pervasive method.

Memphis State—Peer review of courses; and examinations in substantive law courses include professional responsibility components.

New Mexico—Through joint preparation of syllabi by advocacy and clinical faculty.

Pontifical Catholic University of Puerto Rico—Coverage of ethical issues must be included as an objective of every course.

Stanford—Monitored by the dean.

In addition, three law schools reported that the monitoring was done by a combination of reviews of course materials by the school's curriculum committee and class visitations by deans or other members of the faculty.

Interest in the pervasive method appears to be increasing. Seven law schools (University of California–Berkeley, Cornell, Duke, Fordham, Minnesota, Stanford, and Texas) indicated that they have recently received Keck Foundation grants designed to increase the amount of pervasive coverage in their curriculums. In addition, two law schools (Georgetown and Villanova) have recently adopted long-range plans which list increasing the focus on the pervasive system as one of the school's major goals.

There were many interesting suggestions of ways to stimulate increased coverage of legal ethics and professionalism issues by law schools. As expressed in the reply from Vanderbilt University School of Law, the most important ingredient of any such program is a faculty who think that legal ethics and professionalism are important and are willing to do the additional work necessary to implement the curriculum changes adopted as part of the program.

The most frequently mentioned measure was the suggestion that additional course-specific materials on ethics and professionalism be developed. There was a split of opinion, however, over whether these materials should be incorporated into standard casebooks or should be separately published. Many of those who thought the incorporation concept was the best approach suggested that law book publishers should be informed of the need for such materials and encouraged to seek out authors who would be willing to prepare them. Professor Deborah L. Rhode's PROFESSIONAL RESPONSIBILITY—ETHICS BY THE PERVASIVE METHOD (1994), which presents ethical and professionalism issues in the context of ten substantive law areas (civil procedure, constitutional law, contracts, corporations, criminal law and procedure, evidence and trial advocacy, family law, property, tax and torts), is the first set of multiple course-specific materials to be published.

Several of the replies mentioned the desirability of implementing a pervasive approach in the first-year substantive law courses.

Several others mentioned the possibility of a first-year course or series of orientation lectures dealing with professionalism issues. A very thoughtful letter from the Associate Dean for Academic Affairs of Brooklyn Law School combining both these approaches is attached as Exhibit 4.

The following is a representative list of the other suggestions made in the replies to the questionnaire:

- adopt a mandatory pervasive approach in all courses;
- increase the credit hours in existing courses to accommodate coverage of ethical and professionalism issues;
- make ethics and professionalism issues mandatory in all clinical and legal skills courses;
- develop mini-courses or a series of lectures on ethics and professionalism issues for substantive law courses which will be taught by the professors who regularly teach the basic legal ethics course;
- develop advanced courses and seminars on ethics and professionalism;
- produce additional video materials suitable for law school courses dealing with ethics and professionalism issues;
- develop more course materials that incorporate non-traditional teaching methodologies such as storytelling, role-playing and the use of movies and interactive videos;
- rotate all the faculty through the basic legal ethics course;
- encourage greater use of the pervasive method in faculty retreats, faculty colloquia and the like;
- establish a committee (e.g., a faculty development committee) which has as part of its assignment the implementation of a program designed to increase the coverage of ethics and professionalism issues in the curriculum;
- appoint a faculty committee to study the pervasive concept and to make recommendations for its implementation in the curriculum;
- greater use of practitioners and judges as speakers at colloquia, symposia, town hall meetings and the like where the principal focus is professionalism;
- provide support and rewards for faculty who use the pervasive system in their courses;
- the ABA should sponsor an annual law school competition in the fields of ethics and professionalism (the person responding apparently was unaware of the E. Smythe Gambrell Professionalism awards);

- provide a summer reading list on ethics and professionalism issues (e.g., *To Kill a Mockingbird*) to incoming students;
- establish a mentoring program for law students involving the faculty and practitioners;
- establish an Inns of Court involving the law school and the local bar;
- establish mandatory and voluntary *pro bono* programs for law students;
- expand externship and law firm clerking opportunities for law students;
- conduct a survey of existing courses to determine the extent of ethics and professionalism coverage in the curriculum;
- greater stress given to the importance of faculty, judges and practitioners as role models for law students;
- the ABA and AALS should take a greater leadership role in promoting professionalism and the pervasive method; and
- law school deans should aggressively promote increased coverage of ethics and professionalism issues in the curriculum and in extracurricular activities.

APPENDIX B • EXHIBIT 1

Brigham Young University J. Ruban Clark School of Law
First Year Legal Ethics Progam
Course Descriptions

Public Interest Law

A study of lawyers' responsibilities and opportunities to use their specialized training to assist members of the public who are not adequately represented, including an examination of various legal issues commonly encountered in *pro bono* and public interest work. The course will help students prepare themselves to meet these vital legal needs.

Public Interest Externship and LAW HELP Externship

Students are able to earn one credit for each 50 hours of work performed in an approved public interest externship or in one of the LAW HELP *Pro Bono* Externships. LAW HELP *pro bono* projects have included mediation, a Spanish-speaking *pro bono* project, domestic relations, and helping the elderly and disabled. Public interest positions include judicial clerkships, Utah Legal services, criminal defense, and administrative law positions.

In Class Externship Seminar

The purpose of the seminar is to maximize the externship experience by teaching relevant skills and by providing a structure in which the student rigorously analyzes the externship experience. Each student who registers for the Public Interest Externship or LAW HELP *Pro Bono* Externship must take this seminar during the Fall or Winter semester which is concurrent with or immediately following the externship experience. Credit for this seminar is in addition to the externship credit but the latter will not be awarded without satisfactory completion of this classroom component.

Professional Responsibility

The course is less ethics than the law of lawyering. The primary focus is the Model Rules of Professional Conduct.

Professional Seminar

Fall Semester: Readings and discussion sessions explore the intersections of law, religion, values, and professionalism, and the relations between legal education, the legal system, the practice of law and the roles of lawyers in society. The objective is to consider how lawyers should think and act. There are seven 100-minute sessions.

Winter Semester: There is a series of prominent guest and faculty lectures, open to the entire law school. The series will present a wide range of topics of current interest to law students and lawyers concerning basic issues in law, society and values. There are supplemental readings to be completed and adequate attendance is required. Credit can only be earned once.

Valparaiso University School of Law
First Year Ethics Course

Spring 1994

Dean Gaffney

General Purpose. The purpose of this course is not to make you familiar with all the rules relating to admission to the bar or to discipline of lawyers for infractions of the law governing our profession. Those matters are addressed in a separate course entitled Professional Responsibility that you will take later. Neither is this course meant to tell you how to be good. I am going to work on the assumption that you learned that a long time ago. This course is meant to foster some reflection on your aspirations both as lawyers and as human beings. We do this in an organized way at the beginning of your law school experience because the reasons why you want to be a lawyer are often related to the sort of lawyer and person you will become.

Description of Course Content and Procedure. We will explore five themes in this course, two before the break and two after the break. I will introduce each theme in a lecture on a brief set of readings. In the following week a guest lecturer will also explore the theme. On these two weeks we will meet together in Tabor Auditorium. Then we will view a film as part of the required "reading" of the course. The film will be shown in Tabor on Wednesday and Thursday evenings at 7 P.M., and you may choose to attend on either night. Those who live at a distance from the University may certify that you have rented the film and watched it on your own VCR.

Small Group Meetings. On four occasions we will meet in a smaller group for an hour to discuss your views on four of the themes in the course. To accommodate to some extent your preferences both as to scheduling and as to the makeup of the groups, you may sign up on a first-come, first-served basis until noon on Friday, January 14. Those who are in Section__ will need to select a session that does not conflict with your Civil Procedure class on Wednesday. The sign up sheets are with my secretary, Ms. Terry Little. If you do not sign up by Friday, I will assign you randomly to a group. Your written assignment must be handed in to your group leader by noon on the Monday following the film, and you should be prepared to discuss the readings on the theme (including the film) in your group. The meeting in the small group replaces the class meeting in Tabor on that week. The calendar on the opposite side reflects these commitments.

Requirements. You are required to read the assigned materials and to participate in all the class sessions, film sessions, and small group meetings described above. In addition, you must write five short papers (no more than two pages, double spaced) articulating your own personal statement on the themes of the course. The course will be graded Satisfactory-Unsatisfactory. I will assume that all of you will complete all of the assignments and get a grade of Satisfactory. If, however, someone gets a grade of Unsatisfactory, it may be changed into a grade of Satisfactory by completing further assignments that I will make.

Punctuality. Since one of the virtues of a good lawyer is punctuality, no one will receive a Satisfactory grade unless all four assignments are handed in on time. Exceptions to this rule will be granted only for a serious reason explained in writing before the due date.

Civility. Since one of the goals of this course is to learn to collaborate courteously with opponents at the bar, I also attach a copy of the Standards for Professional Conduct adopted by the Seventh Circuit. These standards will serve as a model for all communications during this course. If I determine, after appropriate process, that a serious infraction of these standards has occurred in this course, the penalty will be that a grade of Satisfactory may be earned only by further readings that I will assign, as well as further written reflection on these readings that satisfies me that the offender has grasped the nature of the offense that is caused by incivility.

Sample Professional Seminar Reading Assignments

1. *Law School: The Socratic Method, Uncertainty, and Ambiguity.*
   Professional Seminar Course Information.
   Professional Seminar Statement of Goals and Objectives.
   Bruce C. Hafen, *On Dealing with Uncertainty.*
   Roger C. Cramton, *The Ordinary Religion of the Law School Classroom.*

2. *Law School: Performance, Competition, and Stress.*
   Bruce C. Hafen, *Two Cheers for Excellence.*
   James D. Gordon III, *How Not to Succeed in Law School.*

3. *The Role of Lawyers.*
   Roger C. Cramton, *Why Defend the Guilty?*
   Dallin H. Oaks, *Bridges.*

4. *Litigation and Religious Values.*
   Dallin H. Oaks, *Litigation.*
   David G. Campbell, *Christianity and the Mad Dog Litigator.*

5. *Professionalism.*
   Bruce C. Hafen, *To Beginning Law Students on Professionalism.*
   Tremors in the Realm of Giants.

6. *Honesty.*
   Steven Brill, *Death of a Career.*
   David A. Kaplan, *Sweet Sentiment.*
   Dallin H. Oaks, *Gospel Teachings About Lying.*

7. *Balancing Family, Church, and Career.*
   Spencer W. Kimball, *The False Gods We Worship.*
   Richard Tice, *Greed: When Enough Is Not Enough.*

Reading Certificate

THEME ONE: ETHICS AS VIRTUE AND RESPONSIBILITY

Jan 11	Lecture (Gaffney) What is Ethics? What is Virtue? What is Responsibility?
Jan 18	Lecture (Gaffney) The Role of Community in Learning about [sic] Virtue
Jan 19 & 20, 7 P.M.	Film: "To Kill a Mockingbird"
Jan 25, 26, & 27	Small Group Discussions

THEME TWO: COURTESY AND CIVILITY IN THE PRACTICE OF LAW

Feb 1	Lecture (Gaffney) "The Adversarial Ethic and its Limits"
Feb 8	Guest Lecture (Judge William J. Bauer) "The Requirements of Civility"
Feb 9 & 10, 7 P.M.	Film: "Class Action"
Feb 15, 16, & 17	Small Group Discussions

THEME THREE: PROFESSIONALISM AND THE LAW GOVERNING LAWYERS

Feb 22	Lecture (Professor Shaffer) "The American Bar Association Project on Professionalism"
Mar 1	Lecture (Professor Ehren) "The Law Governing Lawyers"

THEME FOUR: COURAGE, SERENITY, AND WISDOM IN THE PRACTICE OF LAW

Mar 15	Lecture (Gaffney) "The Courage to Change the Things We Can"
Mar 22	Guest Lecture (Judge Jack Allen) "The Serenity to Accept the Things We Cannot Change"
Mar 23 & 24, 7 P.M.	Film: "The Verdict"
Mar 29, 30, & 31	Small Group Discussions

THEME FIVE: EXCLUSION AND INCLUSION IN THE PRACTICE OF LAW

Apr 5	Guest Lecture (Professors Dooley, Lind, & Whitton)
	Exclusion and Inclusion of Women in the Practice of Law
Apr 8, 4 P.M.	Chapel Seegers Lecture (Professor Babcock & Justice O'Connor)
Apr 12	Guest Lecture (Professors Carter & Hatcher)
	Exclusion and Inclusion of Minorities in the Practice of Law
Apr 13 & 14, 7 P.M.	Film: "Separate But Equal"
Apr 19, 20 & 21	Small Group Discussions

APPENDIX B · EXHIBIT 3

Campbell University Norman Adrian Wiggins School of Law
Professionalism Lecture Series
Faculty Moderator: Dean Patrick K. Hetrick

This lecture series is required of all first year law students. It constitutes the first stage of each student's professional responsibility obligation as future members of the legal profession. Fourteen lectures are scheduled throughout the first year of study on topics related to professionalism, ethics, the fundamental values of the legal profession, issues of gender and race in the profession, public service, public interest law, the lawyer's responsibility to serve others, and leadership. The lectures will be presented by leaders in the legal profession, justices and judges, leaders in the state and federal governments, the dean and associate deans, and members of the law faculty. Students will have an opportunity to meet with many guest lecturers either before or after each lecture at an informal reception. Because the obligation to attend is a matter of professional responsibility, no academic credit is given for this lecture series.

The Professionalism Lecture Series will address and explore the following three values set forth in what is known as "the MacCrate Report"[1]:
- Promoting justice, fairness and morality in one's own daily practice;
- Contributing to the profession's fulfillment of its responsibility to ensure that adequate legal services are provided to those who cannot afford to pay for them; and,
- Contributing to the profession's fulfillment of its responsibility to enhance the capacity of law and legal institutions to do justice.

Values addressed and explored will also reflect Campbell's Christian mission and tradition. The effect of Judeo-Christian values on the manner in which lawyers conduct themselves, an analysis of the legal profession from the perspective of stewardship, and the concept of spiritual fulfillment as a practicing lawyer will also be explored.

In addition, each Professionalism Lecture Series lecture will be treated like an appearance in court. Students will be asked to dress in a professional manner appropriate for a court appearance.

---

[1] *Legal Education and Professional Development—An Educational Continuum*, Report of The Task Force on Law Schools and the Profession: Narrowing the Gap, American Bar Assoc. Section of Legal Education and Admissions to the Bar (July, 1992).

Heroes Aren't Hard to Find: The Idea Behind Campbell's Professionalism Lecture Series*

Patrick K. Hetrick, Dean,
Norman Adrian Wiggins School of Law

To stimulate her young pupils, a first-grade teacher in Hornet County arranged to take her class on an educational tour of a local farm. But one perceptive small boy saw right through her scheme. "Don't look, don't look" he warned his buddy as they exited the school bus into the midst of barns, farm animals, pasture and fields of crops. "If we look we'll have to tell about it tomorrow." There is an element of "don't look, don't look" in the day-to-day study of law. First year law students become so emersed [*sic*] in the daily fare of contracts, torts, property law, criminal law and civil procedure and the inescapable concern and preparation for final examinations that their very existence becomes one of dealing with the trees and not the forest of the legal profession.

It is true that a course in ethics in one form or another is taught at all law schools, and that is good. But ethics and even the broader realm of "professional responsibility" tend to be specific do's and don'ts courses with an emphasis on the don'ts. There needs to be some time in the three years of legal education when law students can sit back in class, relax, not be required to recite, and not be held responsible for regurgitating back information received when final exam time comes. There needs to be a "time out" from the rat race of law study when law students can be exposed to and think about the big picture of the legal profession.

The big picture is inextricably intertwined with the concept of professionalism. What does it mean in positive terms to be a member of a learned profession like the legal profession? Above and beyond necessary educational expeditions into the rules all law students need to be aware of in the ethics course, what can be done to cause students to climb to a high plateau and view all there is to see in the panorama we call the legal profession?

Campbell's answer is a new requirement at the law school that all students participate in what is called the "Professionalism Lecture Series" (PLS). What is the PLS about? It's about leaders in the legal profession coming to campus and sharing their thoughts on what it means to be a "lawyer" in the complete sense of that word. And as the first title to this column indicates, heroes aren't hard to find. During seven lectures scheduled in each semester of the first year curriculum, selected "heroes" and "leaders" of the legal profession are invited to Campbell to have lunch with students, present a lecture and then answer questions from the students.

A brief summary of the most recent speakers in the PLS at Campbell will give meaning to the above general description:
- Judge Elizabeth McCrodden of the North Carolina Court of Appeals spoke in the PLS in September. Using the famous and controversial Sacco-Vanzetti case, the seven-year case from the 1920's in which

---

* From *The Campbell Law Observer* (Nov. 1993). Reprinted by permission.

two Italian immigrants with anarchist beliefs were convicted of murder in a shoe factory payroll robbery, Judge McCrodden explored the historic role of courts and the legal profession in confronting racial and other forms of discrimination. Were Sacco and Vanzetti guilty, or were they innocent victims of a legal system prejudiced by their backgrounds and beliefs? Judge McCrodden spoke openly about difficult issues and challenged the law students to make themselves aware of these issues.

- The following week, Susan Olive, president of the North Carolina Association of Women Attorneys, spoke in the PLS on a wide range of issues: professionalism, civility in the practice of law, the status of women in the legal profession, professional obligations of an attorney in drafting contracts, the counseling aspect of being a lawyer and the responsibility of lawyers to set good examples in public and in private.
- The next PLS speaker was Allan Head, executive director of the North Carolina Bar Association. Allan spoke on "leadership" and the responsibilities and attributes of an effective leader. His talk included nuts-and-bolts matters such as communication skills, the effective chairing of professional meetings and rules for being a good bar leader. Campbell's image of the ideal law graduate includes the concept of leadership in one's community and profession. Allan's message was therefore most appropriate.
- On October 26, Julius L. Chambers, distinguished civil rights attorney and chancellor of North Carolina Central University will be the featured speaker. His appearance is made possible by the North Carolina Bar Association's Professionalism Speaker Series, funded by a gift to the NCBA in honor of Judge James Bryan McMillan.

As mentioned above, the Professionalism Lecture Series is required of all first year law students. Borrowing from the ABA "MacCrate Report,"[1] the PLS addresses and explores the following three values:
- Promoting justice, fairness and morality in one's daily practice;
- Contributing to the profession's fulfillment of its responsibility to ensure that adequate legal services are provided to those who cannot afford to pay for them; and
- Contributing to the profession's fulfillment of its responsibility to enhance the capacity of law and legal institutions to do justice.

Values addressed in the lecture series also reflect Campbell's Christian mission and tradition. The effect of Judeo-Christian values on the manner in which lawyers conduct themselves, an analysis of the legal profession from the perspective of stewardship, and the concept as [*sic*] spiritual fulfillment as a practicing lawyer are examples of values that can be explored.

---

[1] *Legal Education and Professional Development An Educational Continuum* Report of The Task Force on Law Schools and the Profession: Narrowing the Gap, American Bar Association Section of Legal Education and Admissions to the Bar (July. 1992).

Because the students' obligation to attend each lecture is presented to them as a matter of professional responsibility, no academic credit is given for the PLS. In addition, each lecture is treated as a court appearance, and students are required to dress appropriately.

It is a privilege to serve as moderator of this important new addition to Campbell's law school curriculum. I know that these lectures will help to provide our students with a vision of what it really means to be a professional. I close this "dean's column" by publicly thanking the judges, lawyers and leaders in the legal profession who are helping to enhance the future of our law students as members of a learned profession by taking the time to travel to Bules Creek and share their thoughts on professionalism with our students.

Lawyers and the Law Firm
Spring 1995 Laboratory Schedule

Laboratory No. 1 Thursday, Jan. 5	Regulation of the Bar; Guest Speaker: Tom Lunsford, Executive Director, The North Carolina State Bar
Laboratory No. 2 Thursday, Jan. 12	Interpersonal Skills: Interviewing and Counseling, Giving and Receiving Feedback, and Introduction to Interviewing Exercise (Complete exercise at discretion and complete report form prior to class on Monday, Jan. 16)
Laboratory No. 3 Thursday, Jan. 19	Review of interviewing exercise and of compilation of reports
Laboratory No. 4 Thursday, Jan. 26	Competence and Knowledge of Self and Others: Campbell Interest and Skill Survey (CISS) feedback session
Laboratory No. 5 Thursday, Feb. 2	Competence and Knowledge of Self and Others: Management Styles Workshop
Laboratory No. 6 Thursday, Feb. 9	Competence and Knowledge of Self and Others: MBTI workshop
Laboratory No. 7 Thursday, Feb. 16	Drafting exercises: partnership agreement provision
Laboratory No. 8 Thursday, Feb. 23	Drafting exercises: affidavit supporting motion for summary judgment
Laboratory No. 9 Thursday, Mar. 2	Trends in the Profession and the North Carolina Quality of Life Survey
Laboratory No. 10 Thursday, Mar. 16	Introduction to Legal Ethics: Presentations by lawyers representing different segments of the bar
Laboratory No. 11 Thursday, Mar. 23	Representing Clients in Questionable Business Transactions; Guest Speaker: Jim Williams
Laboratory No. 12 Thursday, Mar. 30	Representing Criminal Defendants: Guest Speaker: Roger Smith

Laboratory No. 13 **Wed., Apr. 12** **3:00–5:00 P.M.**	Negotiation and Alternative Dispute Resolution exercises; interview witnesses for disciplinary hearing
Laboratory No. 14 Thursday, Apr. 19	Settlement conference and report of proposal or lack thereof (scheduled at discretion) followed by defense and prosecution of disciplinary hearing at time and in courtroom docketed
Laboratory No. 15 As scheduled during semester	Visit to Harnett County Register of Deeds office, with emphasis on conveyances of partnership property

Lawyers and the Law Firm
Spring 1994 Syllabus

Assignment:
Introduction to the Course

I. INTRODUCTION

A. BASIC AGENCY CONCEPTS

Class No. 1 Monday, Jan. 3	Materials, pp. 1–4; Supplement, A Model of the Legal Professionalization Process.

B. THE NATURE OF THE FIRM

Class No. 2 Tuesday, Jan. 4	Materials, pp. 4–17.

C. FIDUCIARY DUTIES

Class No. 3 Wednesday, Jan. 5	Materials, pp. 18–30.

II. AGENCY CONCEPTS AND LINES OF REASONING

A. AUTHORITY

Class No. 4 Monday, Jan. 10	Materials, pp. 31–40; Supplement, Considerations Relating to Business Form.
Class No. 5 Tuesday, Jan. 11	Materials, pp. 40–52.

B. UNDISCLOSED PRINCIPALS

Class No. 6 Wednesday, Jan. 12	Materials, pp. 52–58.

C. CONCEPTS OF INHERENT AUTHORITY AND INHERENT AGENCY POWER

Class No. 7 Monday, Jan. 17	Materials, pp. 59–62.

D. TERMINATION OF AGENCY RELATIONSHIPS

Class No. 8 Tuesday, Jan. 18	Materials, pp. 63–81.

Class No. 9 Wednesday, Jan. 19	Materials, pp. 81–83; Supplement, DAG Matrix and lines of reasoning.

III. LAWYERS AND OTHERS IN PARTNERSHIPS

A. DETERMINING THE EXISTENCE OF PARTNERSHIPS

Class No. 10 Monday, Jan. 24	Materials, pp. 83–88; Scan G.S. Ch. 59; Read G.S. 59–31 through –38 and –46.
Class No. 11 Tuesday, Jan. 25	Materials, pp. 88–95.

B. RIGHTS AND DUTIES OF PARTNERS AMONG THEMSELVES

Class No. 12 Wednesday, Jan. 26	Materials, pp. 96–107; G.S. 59–48 through –53.

1. FIDUCIARY DUTIES

Class No. 13 Monday, Jan. 31	Materials, pp. 108–132.

2. COVENANTS NOT TO COMPETE

Class No. 14 Tuesday, Feb. 1	Materials, pp. 132–172. Sections meet in combined class at 1:00 P.M.

3. INDEMNIFICATION

Class No. 15 Tuesday, Feb. 1	Materials, pp. 172–179. Sections meet in combined class at 2:00 P.M.; class will not meet on Wednesday, Feb. 2

C. PARTNERSHIP PROPERTY

Class No. 16 Monday, Feb. 7	Materials, pp. 180–188; G.S. 59–54 through –58.
Class No. 17 Tuesday, Feb. 8	Materials, pp. 188–195.

D. RELATIONS OF PARTNERS TO PERSONS DEALING WITH THE PARTNERSHIP

Class No. 18 Wednesday, Feb. 9	Materials, pp. 195–205; G.S. 59–39 through –47.
Class No. 19 Monday, Feb. 14	Materials, pp. 205–214.
Class No. 20 Tuesday, Feb. 15	Materials, pp. 214–219.

E. DISSOLUTION AND WINDING UP

Class No. 21 Wednesday, Feb. 16	Materials, pp. 219–226; G.S. 50–59 through –73.
Class No. 22 Monday, Feb. 21	Materials, pp. 227–233.

Class No. 23
Tuesday, Feb. 22

Materials, pp. 233–243.

F. GENDER DISCRIMINATION

Class No. 24
Wednesday, Feb. 23

Materials, pp. 243–292; Supplement, *National Law Journal* article.

G. LIMITED PARTNERSHIPS

Class No. 25
Monday, Feb. 28

Materials, pp. 292–306; Scan G.S. 59–101 through –1106. Review Supplement, Considerations Relating to Business Form.

Class No. 26
Tuesday, Mar. 1

Materials, pp. 306–316; G.S. 59–303 and –1001 through –1006; Supplement, letter from Harold Feder re. *Moore* case.

IV. SECURITIES REGULATION

Class No. 27
Wednesday, Mar. 2

Materials, pp. 316–328; Scan G.S. Chapter 78A; Read G.S. 78A–8 and –17; Supplement, excerpts from 1933 and 193 Acts.

V. THE VALUES AND BEHAVIOR OF LAWYERS: LEGAL ETHICS

Class No. 28
Monday, Mar. 14

Materials, pp. 329–332. In *West*, scan ABA Code of Professional Responsibility and Rules of Professional Conduct. Read North Carolina Rules of Professional Conduct (NCRPC), *Scope* and *Preamble*.

A. THE PROFESSION AND THE PUBLIC

1. MAINTAINING INTEGRITY AND AVOIDING APPEARANCES OF IMPROPRIETY

Class No. 29
Tuesday, Mar. 15

NCRPC Canons I, VIII and IX; Materials, pp. 333–341.

2. UNAUTHORIZED PRACTICE

Class No. 30
Wednesday, Mar. 16

NCRPC Canon III; Materials, pp. 341–348.

B. CLIENT-LAWYER RELATIONSHIPS

1. COMPETENCE

Class No. 31
Monday, Mar. 21

NCRPC Canon VI; Materials, pp. 348–352.

2. CLIENT CONFIDENCES

Class No. 32
Tuesday, Mar. 22

NCRPC Canon IV and Canon VII, Rules 7.1 and 7.2; Materials, pp. 352–365.

Class No. 33
Wednesday, Mar. 23

Materials, pp. 365–377.

3. ZEALOUS REPRESENTATION WITHIN THE BOUNDS OF THE LAW

Class No. 34
Monday, Mar. 28

NCRPC Canon VII; Materials, pp. 377–401.

Class No. 35
Tuesday, Mar. 29

NCRPC Canon VII, Rules 7.3–7.10.

4. CONFLICTS OF INTEREST

Class No. 36
Wednesday, Mar. 30

NCRPC Canon V; Materials, pp. 401–405.

Class No. 37
Monday, Apr. 4

Materials, pp. 405–419.

C. BUSINESS ASPECTS OF PRACTICE AND THE AVAILABILITY OF LEGAL SERVICES

Class No. 38
Tuesday, Apr. 5

NCRPC Canon II; Materials, pp. 419–428.
NCBA Economic Survey.

Class No. 39
Wednesday, Apr. 6

Materials, pp. 428–440.

Class No. 40
Monday, Apr. 11

NCRPC Canon X; review assignment for Class No. 20.

D. THE DISCIPLINARY PROCESS

Class No. 41
Tuesday, Apr. 12

Scan *Red Book*, on reserve in Library, and relate to Supplement, Davis, *Disciplinary Process Flow Chart*.

E. REVIEW AND PREVIEW

Class No. 42
Wednesday, Apr. 13

Materials, pp. 440–458.

Class No. 43
Monday, Apr. 18

Read G.S. 59–45 and –84.1 through –84.3 and 66–68 through –72. Supplement, Isom-Rodriquez, *Limiting the Perils of Partnership* and Supplement, Considerations Relating to Business Form. Scan G.S. Ch. 55B and Ch. 57C.

Class No. 44
Tuesday, Apr. 19

Catchup and review

APPENDIX B · EXHIBIT 4

BROOKLYN LAW SCHOOL
250 JORALEMON STREET

BROOKLYN, NEW YORK 11201

August 2, 1994

William B. Powers
Assistant Consultant
Office of the Consultant on Legal Education
American Bar Association
Indianapolis, Indiana 46202

Re: Survey on Professionalism

Dear Mr. Powers:

I am writing this letter to amplify some of my responses to your Survey on Professionalism. We at Brooklyn Law School have been devoting considerable thought and energy to the matters that are the subject of the Survey, and I wanted to take a few moments to elaborate on our activities.

1. We offer several sections of the more traditional style of course in ethics, titled Legal Profession, which is a requirement of graduation. Most of these sections focus on surveying the basic rules of professional responsibility. One section, however, which is taught by an adjunct who is Chief Counsel to the Disciplinary Committee in Manhattan, approaches the material from the perspective of the practitioner of criminal law and the unique ethical issues that tend to be raised in that context. Another section, taught by a member of our full-time faculty, brings a wide variety of materials to bear on the issues and problems of professional ethics and responsibility.

In addition, we regularly offer seminars on professional responsibility, taught by a full-time faculty member. These classes do satisfy the Legal Profession course requirement, but they are elective in the sense that students who take them have elected to explore the issues in a particularly intense and wide ranging fashion.

2., 3., and 4. We are in the midst of some very promising developments at the law school that bear on the issues of teaching legal ethics and professionalism on a pervasive basis throughout the curriculum. Faculty members are clearly encouraged to do so, and many of our professors who teach required first year courses have started to integrate ethics issues into those courses. For example, one of our Civil Procedure professors reports that she seeks out a number of opportunities to discuss professionalism and ethics concerns with her students, particularly in the context of pleading requirements and discovery practices and procedures, where such issues arise routinely.

More significantly, this year we formed a new Committee on Teaching Professional Ethics to consider these critical issues of professional and ethical responsibility. The Committee is focusing on discussing modifications to the current curriculum to enhance the law school's commitment to professionalism among students and to increase their sensitivity to ethical issues in the context of legal practice.

5. This Committee has determined that issues of ethics and professionalism should be integrated throughout the course of study. As a first step toward this integration, it decided to focus on developing a compendium of problems that could be used to explore ethical and professionalism issues in each of the first year courses. It is anticipated that these problems will be based on cases or other materials already included in first year syllabi.

The Committee has also recommended that we develop a program to introduce professionalism and ethical issues during the orientation period for the entering class, perhaps employing techniques used at professional and academic conferences. Our preliminary thinking is that we might design a day-long program in which a selected issue or set of issues would first be presented to the entire class (through panel discussions, videos or the like) and then be the topic of discussions in small workshops led by members of the faculty.

The Committee believes that such a program would send a valuable institutional message about the importance of professionalism and ethical issues, and lay the groundwork for their further consideration throughout the curriculum.

I appreciate the opportunity to share with you in detail some of the exciting things we have been doing at Brooklyn Law School to address the issues and requirements of professionalism.

With all best wishes.

Sincerely,

Joel M. Gora
Associate Dean for
Academic Affairs,
Professor of Law

Appendix C

Report on State and Local Bar Associations Professionalism Survey

A. Introduction
B. Professionalism and Civility Codes
C. Professionalism Program

A. Introduction

The 1994 Bar Activities Inventory Survey conducted by the American Bar Association Division of Bar Services asked whether a state or local bar association had adopted (1) a professionalism or civility code or (2) a professionalism program. Thirty state bar associations and sixty-nine local bar associations indicated that they had a professionalism or civility code and fifteen state bar associations and twenty-six local bar associations indicated that they had an ongoing professionalism program.

A letter requesting detailed information about these codes and programs was sent to all of these bar associations in mid-November 1994. Fifty-two bar associations (seventeen state and thirty-five local) sent a copy of their professionalism or civility codes and ten bar associations (five state and six local) sent materials on their professionalism programs. Several other bar associations have submitted professionalism reports indicating that they are planning on expanding their professionalism programs.

B. Professionalism and Civility Codes

The principal difference between professionalism and civility codes is that as a general rule the civility codes deal exclusively with appropriate behavior in the context of litigation whereas the existing professionalism codes for the most part include material on a lawyer's duties to the legal system (*pro bono* obligations and the like) and to clients as well as litigation etiquette. The 1992 Standards for Professional Conduct adopted by the Seventh Federal Judicial Circuit, attached as Exhibit 1, represent a fairly typical civility code. The Travis County (Texas) Customs and Practices for Lawyers Statement, attached as Exhibit 2, is fairly typical of the existing professionalism codes.

There are a variety of names and formats for these codes, all of which have apparently been promulgated since the publication in 1986 of the Report of the Commission on Professionalism to the Board of Governors and the House of Delegates of the American Bar Association entitled ". . . In the Spirit of Public Service: A Blueprint for the Rekindling of Lawyer Professionalism," known as the Stanley Commission Report (Justin A. Stanley of Mayer, Brown & Platt in Chicago was chairman of the Commission). Sometimes these codes are referred to as standards, customs and practices, or guides. Often they are referred to as creeds. As a general rule the creeds are first-person pledges by lawyers to abide by the designated standards.

All of these codes are essentially aspirational in nature and are designed to encourage behavior that is above the minimum standards set by the ethical disciplinary rules and the usual court rules that govern lawyers. In fact, many of the professionalism codes, particularly the earlier codes, are very short statements that are essentially a restatement of the aspirational statements in the canons of the ABA Model Code of Professional Responsibility. Most of the more recently adopted codes, however, will describe specific behavior which is deemed to be appropriate (or inappropriate) in addition to the aspirational statements. See Exhibits 1 and 2. A few are very specific and directive. See the Northampton County Bar Association (Easton, Pennsylvania) Guide to Conduct and Etiquette at the Bar, attached as Exhibit 3.

Although these codes cannot be used as the basis for creating new standards for sanctioning lawyers by disciplinary agencies and courts (See the Preamble to the Seventh Circuit Civility Code in Exhibit 1), they can be used as a form of peer pressure by judges and lawyers to exact conformity. *But see Fox v. Lam*, 632 So.2d 877 (La. App. 1994) (court pointed out that a lawyer's unfounded critical statements about the trial judge violated the Louisiana Supreme Court Code of Professionalism but referred the case to the disciplinary board to determine whether the statements in question were sanctionable as an ethics violation).

C. Professionalism Program

Judging by the small number of replies, state and local bar associations have apparently had a more difficult time devising viable programs designed to increase lawyers' sensitivity to professionalism issues than they have experienced in promulgating professionalism and civility codes. There are, however, several innovative programs in existence.

At least three states, Arizona, Maryland and Virginia, have instituted mandatory professionalism programs for newly admitted lawyers. The Maryland program, for example, is a one-day seminar presented in four locations around the state between the day the bar examination results are published and the day set for the swearing-in ceremony. In addition to the usual ethical issues, this program covers court room etiquette, codes of professionalism, lists of available *pro bono* activities in Maryland, sexual harassment and gender bias issues. A teaching guide includes materials describing the coverage and objectives of each segment of the course. Moreover, special interactive video vignettes have been developed for use in this course. Excerpts from the Maryland materials are attached as Exhibit 4.

The Georgia Supreme Court has established by Court Rule the Chief Justice's Commission on Professionalism. Among the interesting projects undertaken by this Commission are: (1) a series of ten town meetings throughout Georgia designed to determine the concerns of lawyers about the decline of professionalism and suggestions for increasing the level of professionalism among lawyers; and (2) a unique two-hour professionalism program taught each year as part of the orientation program in each of Georgia's law schools. Materials describing these programs are attached as Exhibit 5.

A good example of an integrated on-going professionalism program is the Task Force on Professionalism program developed by the Bar Association of Erie County (Buffalo, New York). This program has mentoring and CLE components, a two-and-one-half-day ethics/professionalism program for newly admitted lawyers and bench/bar conferences to discuss professionalism issues. A letter describing these programs is attached as Exhibit 6.

APPENDIX C · EXHIBIT 1

Proposed Standards for Professional Conduct Within the Seventh Federal Judicial Circuit*

Preamble

A lawyer's conduct should be characterized at all times by personal courtesy and professional integrity in the fullest sense of those terms. In fulfilling our duty to represent a client vigorously as lawyers, we will be mindful of our obligations to the administration of justice, which is a truth-seeking process designed to resolve human and societal problems in a rational, peaceful, and efficient manner.

A judge's conduct should be characterized at all times by courtesy and patience toward all participants. As judges we owe to all participants in a legal proceeding respect, diligence, punctuality, and protection against unjust and improper criticism or attack.

Conduct that may be characterized as uncivil, abrasive, abusive, hostile, or obstructive impedes the fundamental goal of resolving disputes rationally, peacefully, and efficiently. Such conduct tends to delay and often to deny justice.

The following standards are designed to encourage us, judges and lawyers, to meet our obligations to each other, to litigants and to the system of justice, and thereby achieve the twin goals of civility and professionalism, both of which are hallmarks of a learned profession dedicated to public service.

We expect judges and lawyers will make a mutual and firm commitment to these standards. Voluntary adherence is expected as part of a commitment by all participants to improve the administration of justice throughout this Circuit.

These standards shall not be used as a basis for litigation or for sanctions or penalties. Nothing in these standards supersedes or detracts from existing disciplinary codes or alters existing standards of conduct against which lawyer negligence may be determined.

These standards should be reviewed and followed by all judges and lawyers participating in any proceeding in this Circuit. Copies may be made available to clients to reinforce our obligation to maintain and foster these standards.

Lawyers' Duties to Other Counsel

1. We will practice our profession with a continuing awareness that our role is to advance the legitimate interests of our clients. In our dealings with others we will not reflect the ill feelings of our clients. We will treat all other counsel, parties,

---

* Final Report of the Committee on Civility of the Seventh Federal Judicial Circuit, 143 F.R.D. 441, 448 (1992).

and witnesses in a civil and courteous manner, not only in court, but also in all other written and oral communications.

2. We will not, even when called upon by a client to do so, abuse or indulge in offensive conduct directed to other counsel, parties, or witnesses. We will abstain from disparaging personal remarks or acrimony toward other counsel, parties, or witnesses. We will treat adverse witnesses and parties with fair consideration.

3. We will not encourage or knowingly authorize any person under our control to engage in conduct that would be improper if we were to engage in such conduct.

4. We will not, absent good cause, attribute bad motives or improper conduct to other counsel or bring the profession into disrepute by unfounded accusations of impropriety.

5. We will not seek court sanctions without first conducting a reasonable investigation and unless fully justified by the circumstances and necessary to protect our client's lawful interests.

6. We will adhere to all express promises and to agreements with other counsel, whether oral or in writing, and will adhere in good faith to all agreements implied by the circumstances or local customs.

7. When we reach an oral understanding on a proposed agreement or a stipulation and decide to commit it to writing, the drafter will endeavor in good faith to state the oral understanding accurately and completely. The drafter will provide the opportunity for review of the writing to other counsel. As drafts are exchanged between or among counsel, changes from prior drafts will be identified in the draft or otherwise explicitly brought to the attention of other counsel. We will not include in a draft matters to which there has been no agreement without explicitly advising other counsel in writing of the addition.

8. We will endeavor to confer early with other counsel to assess settlement possibilities. We will not falsely hold out the possibility of settlement as a means to adjourn discovery or to delay trial.

9. In civil actions, we will stipulate to relevant matters if they are undisputed and if no good faith advocacy basis exists for not stipulating.

10. We will not use any form of discovery or discovery scheduling as a means of harassment.

11. We will make good faith efforts to resolve by agreement our objections to matters contained in pleadings and discovery requests and objections.

12. We will not time the filing or service of motions or pleadings in any way that unfairly limits another party's opportunity to respond.

13. We will not request an extension of time solely for the purpose of unjustified delay or to obtain a tactical advantage.

14. We will consult other counsel regarding scheduling matters in a good faith effort to avoid scheduling conflicts.

15. We will endeavor to accommodate previously scheduled dates for hearings, depositions, meetings, conferences, vacations, seminars, or other functions that produce good faith calendar conflicts on the part of other counsel. If we have been given an accommodation because of a calendar conflict, we will notify those who have accommodated us as soon as the conflict has been removed.

16. We will notify other counsel and, if appropriate, the court or other persons, at the earliest possible time when hearings, depositions, meetings, or conferences are to be canceled or postponed. Early notice avoids unnecessary travel and expense of counsel and may enable the court to use the previously reserved time for other matters.

17. We will agree to reasonable requests for extensions of time and for waiver of procedural formalities, provided our clients' legitimate rights will not be materially or adversely affected.

18. We will not cause any default or dismissal to be entered without first notifying opposing counsel, when we know his or her identity.

19. We will take depositions only when actually needed to ascertain facts or information or to perpetuate testimony. We will not take depositions for the purposes of harassment or to increase litigation expenses.

20. We will not engage in any conduct during a deposition that would not be appropriate in the presence of a judge.

21. We will not obstruct questioning during a deposition or object to deposition questions unless necessary under the applicable rules to preserve an objection or privilege for resolution by the court.

22. During depositions we will ask only those questions we reasonably believe are necessary for the prosecution or defense of an action.

23. We will carefully craft document production requests so they are limited to those documents we reasonably believe are necessary for the prosecution or defense of an action. We will not design production requests to place an undue burden or expense on a party.

24. We will respond to document requests reasonably and not strain to interpret the request in an artificially restrictive manner to avoid disclosure of relevant and non-privileged documents. We will not produce documents in a manner designed to hide or obscure the existence of particular documents.

25. We will carefully craft interrogatories so they are limited to those matters we reasonably believe are necessary for the prosecution or defense of an action, and we will not design them to place an undue burden or expense on a party.

26. We will respond to interrogatories reasonably and will not strain to interpret them in an artificially restrictive manner to avoid disclosure of relevant and non-privileged information.

27. We will base our discovery objections on a good faith belief in their merit and will not object solely for the purpose of withholding or delaying the disclosure of relevant information.

28. When a draft order is to be prepared by counsel to reflect a court ruling, we will draft an order that accurately and completely reflects the court's ruling. We will promptly prepare and submit a proposed order to other counsel and attempt to reconcile any differences before the draft order is presented to the court.

29. We will not ascribe a position to another counsel that counsel has not taken or otherwise seek to create an unjustified inference based on counsel's statements or conduct.

30. Unless specifically permitted or invited by the court, we will not send copies of correspondence between counsel to the court.

Lawyers' Duties to the Court

1. We will speak and write civilly and respectfully in all communications with the court.

2. We will be punctual and prepared for all court appearances so that all hearings, conferences, and trials may commence on time; if delayed, we will notify the court and counsel, if possible.

3. We will be considerate of the time constraints and pressures on the court and court staff inherent in their efforts to administer justice.

4. We will not engage in any conduct that brings disorder or disruption to the courtroom. We will advise our clients and witnesses appearing in court of the proper conduct expected and required there and, to the best of our ability, prevent our clients and witnesses from creating disorder or disruption.

5. We will not knowingly misrepresent, mischaracterize, misquote, or miscite facts or authorities in any oral or written communication to the court.

6. We will not write letters to the court in connection with a pending action, unless invited or permitted by the court.

7. Before dates for hearings or trials are set, or if that is not feasible, immediately after such date has been set, we will attempt to verify the availability of necessary participants and witnesses so we can promptly notify the court of any likely problems.

8. We will act and speak civilly to court marshals, clerks, court reporters, secretaries, and law clerks with an awareness that they, too, are an integral part of the judicial system.

Travis County Customs and Practices for Lawyers

Preamble

The Travis County Bar Association is committed to prevent the infiltration into the practice in our county of the abusive tactics that have surfaced elsewhere. We believe such tactics are a disservice to the public, harmful to our clients, and demeaning to our profession.

In order to accomplish this goal, we have memorialized the following "Travis County Customs and Practices for Lawyers." We have not tried to be exhaustive nor to spell out too many details. We believe the accomplishment of our goals depends upon the good faith of those practicing law in Travis County; not upon a set of rigid rules. These customs and practices have come into being and survived because Travis County practitioners have accepted their spirit as well as their letter. They should not be treated as a set of rules that lawyers can use and abuse to incite ancillary litigation or arguments over whether or not they have been observed.

A copy of these "Travis County Customs and Practices for Lawyers" shall be provided to every lawyer and judge located in Travis County; to each new lawyer coming to Travis County; and we agree to provide a copy, as soon a practical, to all opposing counsel who have occasion to practice in Travis County.

Our intent is that everyone practicing law in Travis County know these customs and practices and live up to them both in letter and spirit.

Response to the failure by an opponent to abide by these customs and practices should seek to avoid a retaliatory escalation of hostility: lawyers should not engage in unprofessional conduct in retaliation against other unprofessional conduct.

Customs and practices can and do change. They are not written in stone. This written memorial can change as well.

I. Our Legal System

A lawyer owes to the administration of justice personal dignity, integrity, and independence. A lawyer should always adhere to the highest principles of professionalism.

    A.   Respect and Dignity. We uphold the respect and dignity of each member of the bar because we revere the law, the legal system and our profession.

    B.   Honesty. Our word is our bond.

    C.   *Pro Bono.* We dedicate and commit ourselves to an adequate and effective *pro bono* program.

    D.   Education. We are obligated to educate our clients, the public, and other lawyers regarding the spirit and letter of these customs and practices.

E.   Appearance of Impropriety. We always conduct ourselves in such a manner as to avoid even the appearance of impropriety.

F.   Reporting. We report to appropriate authorities fraudulent, deceptive or otherwise illegal conduct by a participant in a proceeding before any tribunal unless constrained by an obligation to preserve the confidence and secrets of a client.

II. Lawyer to Client

A lawyer owes to a client allegiance, learning, skill, and industry. A lawyer shall employ all appropriate legal moves to protect and advance the client's legitimate rights, claims, and objections. A lawyer shall not be deterred by any real or imagined fear of judicial disfavor or public unpopularity, nor be influenced by mere self-interest.

A.   Advice to Clients

1.   We advise our clients of the contents of these customs and practices when undertaking representation.

2.   We advise our clients regarding the availability of mediation, arbitration, and other alternative methods of resolving and settling disputes.

B.   Independent Judgment

1.   We are always conscious of our duty to the judicial system.

2.   We are loyal and committed to our clients' lawful objectives, but we do not permit that loyalty and commitment to interfere with our duty to provide objective and independent advice.

3.   We reserve the absolute right to determine whether to grant accommodations to opposing counsel in all matters that do not adversely affect our clients' lawful objectives.

4.   A client has no right to demand that we engage in abusive or offensive conduct.

5.   We neither encourage nor cause clients or anyone under our control to do anything that would be unethical or improper if done by us.

C.   Proper Conduct on Behalf of Clients

1.   We affirm that among parties and their lawyers civility and courtesy are expected and are not a sign of weakness.

2.   We treat adverse parties and witnesses with fairness and due consideration.

3.   We endeavor to achieve our clients' lawful objectives in business transactions and in litigation as expeditiously and economically as possible.

4.   We do not pursue litigation (or any other course of action) that is without merit and do not engage in tactics that are intended primarily to delay resolution of a matter or to harass or drain the financial resources of the opposing party.

III. Lawyer to Lawyer

A lawyer owes to opposing council, in the conduct of business transactions and the pursuit of litigation, courtesy, candor, cooperation, and scrupulous observance of all agreements and mutual understandings. Ill feelings between clients shall not influence a lawyer's conduct, attitude, or demeanor toward opposing counsel.

A. Courtesy and Punctuality

    1. We are courteous, civil and prompt in oral and written communications and punctual in honori¬g scheduled appearances.

    2. We disagree without being disagreeable. We recognize that effective representation does not require antagonistic or obnoxious behavior.

    3. We do not, without good cause, attribute bad motives or unethical conduct to opposing counsel nor bring the profession into disrepute by unfounded accusations or acrimony toward opposing counsel, parties and witnesses. We are not influenced by any ill feeling between clients. We abstain from any allusion to personal peculiarities or idiosyncrasies of opposing counsel.

    4. We do not ask a witness a question solely for the purpose of harassing or embarrassing the witness.

B. Drafting

    1. We do not quarrel over matters of form or style, but concentrate on matters of substance.

    2. We try to achieve the common goal in the preparation of agreements. We do not include terms neither desired nor insisted upon by any party.

    3. When we purport to identify for other counsel or parties changes we make in documents submitted for their review, we identify all such changes accurately.

    4. We notify opposing counsel, and, if appropriate, the Court or other persons as soon as practicable, when hearings, depositions, meetings, conferences or closings are canceled.

C. Scheduling, Extensions, Cancellations

    1. We do not arbitrarily schedule a deposition, court appearance, or hearing until a good faith effort has been made to schedule it by agreement. If we are unable to contact the other lawyer, we send written correspondence suggesting a time or times that will become operative unless an informal objection is directed to us within a set reasonable time.

    2. We endeavor in good faith to honor previously scheduled trial settings, vacations, seminars or other functions that produce good faith calendar conflicts on the part of opposing counsel. We do not seek accommodation from another member of the Bar for the scheduling of any court setting or discovery unless a legitimate need exists. We do not misrep-

resent conflicts, nor do we ask for accommodation for the purpose of tactical advantage or undue delay.

3. We agree to reasonable requests for extensions of time and for waiver of procedural formalities, provided legitimate objections of our clients will not be adversely affected.

4. We notify opposing counsel, and, if appropriate, the Court or other persons, as soon as practicable, when hearings, depositions, meetings, conferences or closings are canceled.

D. Discovery

1. We make reasonable efforts to conduct all discovery by agreement.

2. We refrain from excessive and abusive discovery.

3. We comply with all reasonable discovery requests. We do not resist discovery requests that are not objectionable. We do not make objections nor give instructions to a witness for the purpose of delaying or obstructing the discovery process. We encourage witnesses to respond to all deposition questions that are reasonably understandable. We do not encourage or cause our witness to quibble about words where their meaning is reasonably clear within the context in which the words are used.

4. We do not seek Court intervention to obtain discovery that is clearly improper and not desirable.

E. Sanctions. We do not seek sanctions or disqualifications unless it is necessary for protection of our clients' lawful objectives or fully justified by the circumstances.

F. Opportunity to Respond

1. We do not serve motions, pleadings or briefs in any manner that unfairly limits another party's opportunity to respond. We furnish opposing counsel copies of all submissions to the Court either contemporaneously or as soon as practical.

2. We do not take advantage, by causing any default or dismissal to be rendered, when we know the identity of an opposing counsel without first making a good faith attempt to inquire about the counsel's intention to proceed.

G. Orders. We promptly submit orders to the Court. We promptly approve the form of orders that accurately reflect the substance of rulings of the Court.

H. Unnecessary Posturing. We avoid argument or posturing through unnecessarily sending copies of correspondence to the Court.

I. Stipulations. We readily stipulate to understand facts in order to avoid needless costs or inconvenience for any party.

J. Request During Trial. During trial we honor reasonable requests of opposing counsel that do not prejudice the rights of our clients or sacrifice tactical advantage.

IV. Lawyer and Judge

Lawyers and judges owe each other respect, diligent order, punctuality, and protection against unjust and improper criticism and attack. Lawyers and judges are equally responsible to protect the dignity and independence of the Court and the profession.

    A. Conduct of Counsel

        1. We always recognize that the position of the judge is the symbol of both the judicial system and administration of justice. We refrain from conduct that degrades that symbol.

        2. We conduct ourselves in Court in a professional manner and demonstrate our respect for the Court and the law.

        3. We respect the rulings of the Court.

        4. We treat counsel, opposing parties, the Court, and members of the Court staff with courtesy and civility.

        5. We do not misrepresent, mischaracterize, misquote or miscite facts or authorities to gain an advantage.

        6. We do no engage in ex parte communications with the Court, the Court's clerks or briefing attorneys, or any other Court personnel. We do not condone or lend ourselves to private influencing by another, of a judge, hearing officer or their personnel on behalf of ourselves or our clients.

    B. Conduct of Court. We give the issues in controversy deliberate, impartial and studied analysis and consideration.

    C. Cooperation Between Court and Counsel

        1. We are considerate of the time constraints and pressures imposed upon the Court, Court staff and counsel in efforts to administer justice and resolve disputes.

        2. We are punctual.

APPENDIX C · EXHIBIT 3

The Northampton County Bar Association Guide to Conduct and Etiquette at the Bar

These guiding principles comprise the considered opinion of the Bench and Bar of Northampton County concerning professional etiquette and are a result of suggestions made by the Bench at the request of the Bar.

1. Lawyers should dress in a fashion consistent with the respect they expect the public to have for their profession. Lawyers should not appear before the Court in overcoats or other wearing apparel designed for outdoor wear. Lawyers who are at the courthouse for reasons other than a Court appearance should nonetheless recognize the courthouse as the center and focus of their professional activity and dress accordingly. The same formality of dress that is appropriate for the courtroom is appropriate for an appearance before a Judge at the Judge's office or in the Judge's chambers.

2. Lawyers should ask permission to address the Court rather than just jumping up and starting to talk. The proper method of requesting such permission is to preface one's remark by the phrase: "May it please the Court . . ."

3. Lawyers should request permission to approach the bench prior to doing so. While at sidebar, lawyers should not rest upon nor "drape themselves" over the bench.

4. Lawyers should first address the Court and opposing counsel before addressing the jury. The proper form of doing this is to first address the Court: "May it please the Court." The Court then acknowledges counsel. Counsel then addresses opposing counsel first: "Mr., Ms., Mrs.,_____," and then "Ladies and Gentlemen of the Jury."

5. Lawyers should always stand when addressing the court. This should be done even at the call of the hearing list and the various trial lists.

6. Lawyers when making objections should stand and state a brief (one word if possible) reason for the objection, such as "Objection: Hearsay." If it is necessary to enlarge the record after an objection, lawyers should approach the bench and quietly, out of the hearing of the jury, state their reasons. They should not present their arguments to the jury but only to the Court.

7. In addressing a witness lawyers should stand behind their desk and if for any reason they want to approach the witness, they should only do so after obtaining the court's permission.

8. When marking exhibits for identification, it is suggested that the courteous way of doing this is to give the exhibit to the court reporter to have the exhibit marked, and to then exhibit it to the court and to opposing counsel. All of these actions should be performed before questions are again directed to the wit-

ness. The court reporter cannot possibly mark an exhibit and record testimony at the same time. Where there are a multitude of exhibits, they should be marked in advance by the court reporter or the lawyers. When possible and not too cumbersome, separate copies of exhibits should be provided for the Court. This permits the original to remain with the court reporter and avoids the problem of lawyers having to search for them on the bench or elsewhere.

9. Lawyers should always keep their voices up and remind their witnesses to do the same.

10. Lawyers should never directly address opposing counsel in Court. Lawyers should directly address only the Court, the jury, and the witnesses.

11. A lawyer should not call any witness, even his or her client, by the witness' first name.

12. Lawyers should limit voir dire questions to the proper purpose of voir dire and should not attempt to instruct the jury as to the law or to argue their case to the jury by means of voir dire questions.

13. As a tactical point, there is a great weight of authority to the effect that cases are won or lost on direct examination. Young lawyers uniformly have a tendency to overdo the cross-examination of witnesses.

14. Motion Court convenes at 9:00 A.M. every day except weekends and holidays. Except for rules to show cause, lawyers should supply to all opposing counsel a copy of the proposed motion and notice of the date the motion is to be presented at least three days prior to presenting the motion. A motion should not be presented to any Judge other than the Motion Judge, nor at any time other than during Motion Court, unless emergency relief is required.

15. Lawyers should be on time for all court appearances, including all calls of the list.

16. Lawyers who have cases on a miscellaneous hearing list should remain immediately available, so that when their case is called they are ready to begin promptly.

17. Lawyers should not initiate conversation with jurors who have served on a jury in a case they were trying.

18. If a lawyer has an uncontested motion or rule to show cause and cannot get to Motion Court, he or she may leave it with the Court Administrator who will present it to the Motion Judge and return it to the lawyer.

19. All lawyers, in accordance with the Court Rules and Rule 1.1 of the Rules of Professional Conduct, should be prepared at all times when they appear before the Court.

20. Lawyers should exhibit courtesy in the courtroom toward opposing counsel as well as to the court and to witnesses.

21. Lawyers should at all times deal with each other honestly and with respect. It is suggested that communication between counsel in the presence of clients and before the court shall be with respect and courtesy—"Treat others as you would have them treat you."

22. Lawyers should be cognizant of the effect of use of gender specific terms when addressing another lawyer. Such language tends to degrade the recipient in the eyes of clients and others.

23. By the very nature of our profession, heated exchanges occur. Threats of physical violence, however, cannot and should not be tolerated or condoned under any circumstances.

24. Whenever possible, trial counsel should include the authority relied upon in points for charge and refrain from unduly repetitious points.

25. Lawyers should wait until *all* of the assignments have been announced on a miscellaneous hearing or argument list before engaging others in conversation or gathering their briefcases, charts, and other paraphernalia and leaving the courtroom.

26. Lawyers should be available in their offices or at the Courthouse to respond to telephone civil status calls at least one-half hour prior to the designated time.

27. Trials or hearings may not be continued without Court approval. Discovery deadlines fixed by court order may not be extended without Court approval. The mere agreement of counsel to a continuance or to an extension is insufficient.

28. The Court's overall view is that it is pleased with the courtroom demeanor of the Northampton County Bar.

29. These guidelines should not be construed as being a criticism of the Bar in general, or of any lawyers in particular, but merely as suggestions to all members of the Bar who are perhaps not aware of these matters.

30. The Court has particularly expressed its satisfaction with the preparedness of counsel at pretrial conferences and will continue to insist that this level of preparedness be maintained.

Revised January 1994

Professionalism Beyond Ethics

A course for new lawyers developed for the Court of Appeals of Maryland by the Maryland State Bar Association with the assistance of the Maryland Institute for Continuing Professional Education of Lawyers, Inc.

History of the Course on Professionalism

Ten years ago, the President of the Maryland State Bar Association appointed the late Stuart Rome, Esquire, as Chair of a Special Committee on Law Practice Quality. The Committee was charged with the task of developing a process of peer review of law practices to enhance the quality of professional services. After several years of study, the Committee concluded that the need to protect the confidentiality of the relationship between an attorney and his or her client was an obstacle to the implementation of a system of peer review. However, the Committee developed a manual for a self survey by a law practice for those lawyers interested in improving the quality of their practice. The manual was published simultaneously by the Maryland State Bar Association and the American Law Institute of the American Bar Association.

The Committee then turned its attention to the increasing dissatisfaction of practicing attorneys with the profession. With the sudden and dramatic changes in our national life, the great increase in the number of lawyers, new economic pressures upon law practices, and the emphasis upon the business aspects rather than the professional side of the lawyer's life, there arose a cry for reform. Lawyers complained about the tyranny of the time sheet, and the Rambo practice of Law.

For a year, under the Chairmanship of James Kramon, the members of the Committee explored circumstances which had led to making the practice of law inhospitable and unrewarding. The Committee found excessive adversarial relationships among attorneys; a loss of civility; the absence of any true mentorship of younger lawyers; and an increasing trend toward specialization in the early years leading to the development of highly competent technicians but not full and accomplished professionals. The findings of the Committee were captured by Mr. Kramon in the December 1986 issue of The Maryland Bar Journal in an article entitled: Lawyers Look At The Practice Of Law—Some Disquieting Observations.

In March 1987, the Committee invited the managing partners of three of Baltimore's largest law firms to discuss the findings of the Committee. We were pleased to learn that they shared our concerns and wished to work with us in addressing the matter. They proposed that the Committee undertake, with their financial assistance, a survey by personal interviews of attorneys to determine the causes of dissatisfaction and possible solutions. The project received the enthusiastic approval of the Board of Governor of the MSBA backed by financial support of both the MSBA and the Maryland Bar Foundation.

The Committee spent approximately a year during which time it raised the necessary funds and entered into discussions with PSYCOR, Inc., of Philadelphia, Pennsylvania, who were eventually employed to assist in the study to be conducted by a series of structured interviews of a number of attorneys to be selected by probability sampling methods. Considerable time was spent in discussing the various concerns and developing the issues to be the subject of the study, as well as the development of a questionnaire and the testing of that questionnaire with attorneys. A representative number of law practices were also solicited who agreed to be a part of the survey. The firms were divided into three sizes: small, consisting of ten or less attorneys; medium, 11 to 49 attorneys; and large, 50 attorneys or over. Out of a potential universe of 1,027 attorneys, 207 were eventually interviewed by 21 graduate students at the University of Maryland School of Social Work and Community Planning. The interviews were held in total confidence and conducted away from the premises of either the law practice or of the Bar Association. Finally, the study was completed and the report was submitted to the Board of Governors of the Maryland State Bar Association on December 30, 1988. The report was entitled: How Attorneys and Law Firms in Maryland's Major Urban Areas View the Quality of Their Professional Lives and Issues Facing the Profession.

On March 17th and March 18th of 1989, a conference of a cross-section of judges and attorneys was held at the Columbia Inn, at the conclusion of which a series of recommendations was adopted. The recommendation ranked third in order of importance was that the Maryland State Bar Association and/or the Court of Appeals should require attendance of attorneys at a seminar or course on professionalism. Soon thereafter, the Board of Governors of the Maryland State Bar Association unanimously agreed to support the concept of a mandatory course on professionalism and ethics to be taken by new lawyers within one to two years after their admission to the Bar.

The State Bar Association formed a committee on Professionalism. The first assignment of the Committee was to assist the officers of the MSBA in persuading the Rules Committee of the Court of Appeals to consider a rule requiring the course. Both the Rules Committee and the Committee on Professionalism worked very diligently in crafting a rule which was practical in achieving the goal of the Maryland Rules of Civil Procedure. Rule 11 requires a person before admission to the Bar to complete a course on legal professionalism.

The Course is given twice annually during the period between the announcement of Bar examination results and the scheduled admission ceremony [*sic*] that the requirement would remain in force for a period of three years from the effective date of the Rule during which time the Court of Appeals shall evaluate the results of the Course requirement to determine whether to extend the requirement.

Table of Contents

APPENDIX C · EXHIBIT 5

Town Hall Meetings
Chief Justice's Commission on Professionalism
Atlanta, Georgia

Creation of the Town Hall Meeting Project

In 1992, the Commission demonstrated that it views the professionalism effort as a statewide, grass roots movement by going to the lawyers and judges throughout the state and listening to their concerns about the profession. Each Town Hall Meeting was planned to include a local sponsoring lawyer and a local sponsoring judge, selected by the Commission for their active role in bench and bar activities and ability to attract participants to the meetings. To initiate the meetings, the Chief Justice of the Georgia Supreme Court sent letters to the prospective sponsoring lawyers, and the President of the Council of Superior Court Judges sent letters to the prospective sponsoring judges (See Sample Letters). As each local sponsor responded to the letters, the Commission's staff worked with the sponsors on plans for each meeting. The meetings were planned to last two hours for which the lawyers attending received two hours of continuing legal education credit, one hour of Ethics and one hour of Professionalism. To the local sponsors the Commission delegated the responsibility to plan the date, time, and place of the meeting to accommodate local needs. The sponsors were encouraged to include a luncheon or reception prior to or following the meeting to promote camaraderie among attendees.

Each local sponsor was asked to identify a number of facilitators for small group discussions sufficient to handle groups of ten or less. The Commission staff developed and sent to each facilitator a memorandum outlining the facilitator's responsibilities (See Facilitators Memo). The Commission staff applied for continuing legal education credit for each meeting and developed and duplicated all of the course materials.

The structure of each of the Town Hall Meetings was uniform (See Sample Agenda). Each meeting began with a welcome from the local sponsoring lawyer, an introduction to the program by the local sponsoring judge, and an explanation of the reason for Town Hall Meetings by the Chief Justice or another justice of the Supreme Court of Georgia. A member of the Commission's staff then gave the program overview and instructions and explained that the main tasks of the meeting were to identify problems and concerns of the local legal community and to elicit ideas about how to approach solutions to these concerns. The participants then went into small groups of not more than ten. Each group was asked to use the first 10–15 minutes in the group to complete, if possible, the entire questionnaire which consisted of seven questions (See Questionnaire). The groups were asked to spend the next 40–45 minutes discussing two questions of the seven on the questionnaire: the "Common Question," and another question which varied from group to group. The "Common Question" dealt with the symptoms of professionalism decline in the community. The basis for asking each group to address this question is the prevailing nation-wide focus on the fact that while lawyers may observe the rules of ethics governing their conduct, lawyers' professionalism, by contrast, is perceived to be in steep decline.

Following the breakout groups, the participants reassembled for the Reporting Out portion of the program, where a representative of each group gave a summary of the group's discussion of the two questions. Summarization and final comments by a Commission staff member or the sponsoring lawyer or judge then completed the program. After the first of the meetings, an article was published in the *State Bar News* to alert the legal community to the state-wide nature of the meetings (See Article).

Following each meeting, the Commission's staff collated the responses on the questionnaires for each meeting and sent a copy of the collation to each participant. It also sent letters of thanks and Certificates of Appreciation to each sponsoring lawyer and judge. The Commission then compiled and summarized in narrative form the collations from each meeting for distribution, exploration, and discussion at the Convocation (See Appendix).

Given the enthusiastic reception and response these meetings enjoyed, the Commission has concluded that it has moved the professionalism effort in this state forward. The challenge before the Commission now is to take the results from the Town Hall Meetings and utilize them to renew the Commission's mandate to inspire lawyers to view the practice of law as a calling in the spirit of service to clients and to the public.

Agenda

Date

(Time)

Town Hall Meeting

"ATTORNEY CONCERNS ABOUT ETHICS AND PROFESSIONALISM"

5:00	Welcome	Program Chair/Sponsoring Lawyer
5:05	Introduction of the Program	Local Sponsoring Judge
5:10	Why Town Hall Meetings?	Chief Justice, Supreme Court of Georgia
5:20	Program Overview and Instructions	Executive Director Chief Justice's Commission on Professionalism
5:25	Transition into Groups	
5:30	Small Group Facilitated Discussions	
6:20	Break	
6.30	Reporting Out	Assistant Director Chief Justice's Commission on Professionalism
6:50	Summarization and Final Comments	Local Sponsoring Judge

Orientations on Professionalism*

Sally Evans Lockwood, Assistant Director
Chief Justice's Commission on Professionalism

To plant the seeds of professionalism at the beginning of law students' careers, the State Bar Committee on Professionalism, chaired by Dana B. Miles of Decatur, created a pilot project called Orientations on Professionalism. The orientations were conducted at the four ABA-accredited law schools in Georgia in August and September of 1993. Each two-hour program consisted of a key-note address by a justice of the Supreme Court of Georgia, followed by a one-hour breakout session where facilitators led students in examining hypotheticals designed to provoke discussion of professionalism and ethical issues. To help bridge the gap between law school and the profession, the Committee focused most of the hypotheticals on issues that arise in the lawyer-client relationship. Facilitators were all members of the Georgia Bar—practicing lawyers, judges, and legal academicians—who volunteered for the project. At each school, students were divided into groups of ten with two facilitators per group. An effort was made to insure geographic, practice area, gender, and race diversity among facilitators. After the breakouts, all of the students and facilitators reconvened for a reporting session where a student from each group reported on that group's resolution of the hypotheticals or reaction to the discussion process. A State Bar officer concluded each program by giving personal reflections on professionalism. The Committee and the Chief Justice's Commission on Professionalism, which provided coordination, staffing, and funding for the programs, hosted a reception for students, facilitators, and faculty to give them an opportunity to meet with each other and follow up group discussions in an informal setting.

The evaluations from the students and the facilitator comments led us to conclude that these sessions were successful in encouraging law students, early in their careers, to gain a better understanding of professionalism and to take a professionalism perspective into their classes on substantive law. One student summed up the program by saying: "From the exercise, I learned that I don't have to discard my personal ethical values in order to become a lawyer." Other comments from unsigned student evaluations, facilitators, and a parent-lawyer appear below.

The American Bar Association Commission on Partnership Programs has selected the State Bar of Georgia Orientations on Professionalism as the recipient of the 1994 American Bar Association/Information America Client Relations Project Award. The award, which carries a cash grant of $3000, was presented to Dana Miles at the Midyear Meeting of the ABA in Kansas City in February. The cash grant will be applied to the 1994 Orientations.

---

* 30 Georgia State Bar Journal 195 (1994). Reprinted by permission of the Georgia State Bar Journal.

The Committee expresses deep appreciation to the 160 justices, judges, lawyers, and legal educators who participated as speakers and facilitators at the 1993 Orientations. Your participation was the key to the success of the programs.

The success of the programs has led each of the law schools to ask the committee to repeat the Orientations in 1994. The committee is already planning next year's programs. If you are interested in participating in the 1994 programs, please contact Terie Latala, Administrative Assistant, Chief Justices's Commission of Professionalism, 800 The Hurt Building, 50 Hurt Plaza, Atlanta, Georgia 30303, (404) 527-8793 or 1-800-334-6865.

Students' Comments

The main thing about this program was that it gave us a focus of how we should act, how we should be—not crass, cold lawyers out to make money—we should be professional, ethical, and moral. To me, all three go hand in hand. By doing this during orientation, it sends the right message.

It was nice to discuss these issues outside a classroom in a small group so that we could express our personal views, as well as our thoughts on professional responsibility. Informal interaction with members of the bench and bar is great, too.

Give a program like this each year! I know I'd look at the hypos (possibly even the same ones) differently as a 2-L and 3-L after more "legal experience." If you offered another program similar to this one, I would attend. This program should only be an introduction to professionalism. As our speaker said, it is a continuing process.

The thing that impressed me was the lawyers and their keen insight. They had scruples to throw at you, and they showed us that there are no easy answers.

Good format. It was nice to get to spend time with practicing attorneys.

Excellent idea—it got me thinking about these complicated issues as a part of everyday lawyering.

Talking with attorneys about real-life situations that they had encountered was the most interesting and informative part.

I think that this program and its focus on what "being a lawyer in 1993 is really like" is extremely beneficial. I would like to see the school sponsor more than just one two-hour conference for my 3 years of education and chosen career. . . . Professionalism and ethics seem to be as relevant to our profession as learning the principles of law and the thought process.

The profession ideally works together, not against one another.

This program enhanced my understanding of professionalism and ethics by clarifying where your duty to the profession and to the facilitation of justice lies in respect to your duty to your client.

I found this program challenging. Not in every dilemma an attorney is faced with is there a cut and dry right or wrong thing to do. I enjoyed considering the hypotheticals.

The facilitators were helpful, informative, knowledgeable, friendly, and argumentative all at the same time.

More "true facts of the outside world" experiences during the very first weeks of law school, like this one, would help us new guys get perspective on our goals quicker.

Facilitators' Comments

I commend whoever did the planning and organizing of our particular group; it presented the perfect contrast between a big firm, city practice and a small town, country practice. John Chandler, a partner with Sutherland, Asbill & Brennan in Atlanta and I were the facilitators for our group and we found that it added a wonderful dimension to the discussion to be able to present our differing legal perspectives based on our different experiences. The students in our group were not shy and we enjoyed a lively discussion on all three hypotheticals. A number of the students approached me afterwards to express their appreciation for our participation, to follow up on points that had been raised in discussions and to ask further questions. Their discussion while in the group and their questions afterwards reinforced my belief that participation in professionalism orientation sessions such as this are needed and useful. I must also say that I enjoyed it every bit as much as the students.

Catherine Harris Helms
Homerville, Georgia

On the way back from lunch I asked the two students I was driving with if they were looking forward to the beginning of classes. One of them responded: "I am kind of depressed. This is not as straightforward as I thought it would be." I am not sure if the student was reflecting upon the professionalism orientation or the overall orientation process. Nonetheless, I truly sense that most of the students were looking at their future practice of law in a way which they have not previously considered.

I think the commission's work with members of the bar is good, but I have noticed that it is sometimes difficult to teach old dogs new tricks. I think you will get a greater return from your investment by directing your efforts at the newer and yet to be members of the profession.

Paul T. Carrol III
Rome, Georgia

[I]t was clear to me that the orientation program at Emory had a significant effect on the students. I observed a sense of relief among the students in learning that the duties of an advocate do not require lawyers to leave their personal values at the courthouse door.

J. Comer Yates
Atlanta, Georgia

I would like to personally thank you for taking such an interest in the education of our law students in order that we can hopefully reverse this trend of unprofessional conduct within the legal profession . . .

I feel this is a start toward a higher level of education in our law school.

Jefferson L. Davis, Jr.
Judge, Superior Court
Cherokee Judicial Circuit
Cartersville, Georgia

I found the program to be a very rewarding experience. The committee's efforts provided not only a benefit to the students, but to the profession itself. I welcome the opportunity to participate in future programs of its nature conducted in Atlanta.

Robert Preston Brown
Atlanta, Georgia

I appreciate all of the good work that is being done in this area. It is important that all of us work to make sure that those who are entering the practice of law are as aware of how strongly many of us feel about what lack of professionalism is doing to our profession. If I can be of any assistance to you, please let me know.

Walter J. Matthews
Judge, Superior Court
Rome Judicial Circuit
Rome, Georgia

I would also like to thank the Chief Justice's Commission of Professionalism for the course in professionalism that my son, Peter Hardy, received at the Emory University School of Law. My son, Peter Hardy, entered the Emory University School of Law as a freshman in August and he was very impressed with the professionalism program that he received at the outset of his legal education.

Thank you very much for helping my son get started in his legal education with a very high regard for professionalism.

W. Marvin Hardy III, Parent
Orlando, Florida

APPENDIX C · EXHIBIT 6

BAR ASSOCIATION OF ERIE COUNTY

1450 STATLER TOWERS
BUFFALO, NEW YORK 14202-3014

November 21, 1994

Harry J. Haynsworth
Dean and Professor of Law
South Illinois University at Carbondale
Carbondale, IL 62901-6804

Dear Dean Haynsworth:

I write in response to your recent request for information about our Association's professionalism program.

Created in 1993, our program is overseen by a Task Force on Professionalism, which is comprised of lawyers and judges representing various courts and areas of law and includes the Presiding Justice of the Appellate Division for the Fourth Judicial Department.

Although the Task Force is relatively new it has accomplished several major tasks and is planning some others.

Mentoring

A formal program of mentoring was established, principally for newly-admitted attorneys, but available also to attorneys at any level of experience who either request it or for whom it is recommended by our Foundation or as a result of disciplinary proceedings. To date about fifty mentors have been assigned and requests continue to be received.

Resource Directory

This is a directory of attorneys organized by areas of practice, size of firm and years of experience. Listing in the directory is open to all members of the Association. The directory was published and distributed to all members of the Association this Summer and is designed to [sic] guidance and practical advice in areas of the law in which a lawyer may be unfamiliar.

Continuing Legal Education

The Task Force identified some professionalism issues: lack of civility in the courts, poor attorney/client relations, poor communications with clients and other lawyers, failure to use retainer letters, failure to distinguish issues, etc. To address these concerns our continuing legal education program now includes practice tips as part of its programming. Representatives from the local disciplinary office are also invited regularly to offer advice on how to avoid disciplinary action. Our monthly newsletter is also used to communicate this information.

Judicial Conference

A program was organized by our presiding justice on how judges should treat litigants and was presented at the annual summer conference held for the judiciary.

New Attorney Primer

A 2½ day program will be offered for the first time in March 1995 for newly-admitted attorneys. This is a collaborative effort with the Courts, Law School, GOLD (Graduates of the Last Decade) and our own Foundation. The first half-day will focus on professionalism topics including a skit on the right and wrong way to communicate with another lawyer on a case; day two will cover how to start and build a law practice and will offer advice from payroll to good advertising practices; day three is a basic "how-to" course in several substantive areas of law and will include forms and check-lists as supplemental material.

Judge/Lawyer Program

Finally, a program is being designed for the Spring of 1995 which will feature a panel of judges from various courts and lawyers to talk about courtroom etiquette. Our program is modeled after a successful program offered during the second circuit judicial conference last July. The program is moderated by a facilitator and works as a forum for the exchange of comments and ideas between judges and lawyers on how to improve courtroom etiquette.

I hope this information will be helpful to you. I am enclosing some of our printed materials. Please feel free to contact me if you need further information.

Very truly yours,

KATHERINE STRONG BIFARO

Executive Director

KSB/tbm

Appendix D

Law Firm Pro Bono Challenge
Statement of Principles*

Recognizing the growing severity of the unmet legal needs of the poor and disadvantaged in the communities we serve, and mindful that major law firms must—in the finest traditions of our profession—play a leading role in addressing these unmet needs, our firm is pleased to join with other firms across the country in subscribing to the following statement of principles and in pledging our best efforts to achieve the voluntary goals described below.

1. Our firm recognizes its institutional obligation to encourage and support the participation by all of its attorneys in *pro bono publico* activities. We agree to promulgate and maintain a clearly articulated and commonly understood firm policy which unequivocally states the firm's commitment to *pro bono* work.

2. To underscore our institutional commitment to *pro bono* activities, we agree to use our best efforts to ensure that, by no later than the close of calendar year 1995, our firm will either:

    (1) annually contribute, at a minimum, an amount of time equal to 5 percent of the firm's total billable hours to *pro bono* work;

    or

    (2) annually contribute, at a minimum, an amount of time equal to 3 percent of the firm's total billable hours to *pro bono* work.

3. In recognition of the special needs of the poor for legal services, we believe that our firm's *pro bono* activities should be particularly focused on providing access to the justice system for persons otherwise unable to afford it. Accordingly, in meeting the voluntary goals described above, we agree that a majority of the minimum *pro bono* time contributed by our firm should consist of the delivery of legal services on a *pro bono* basis to persons of limited means or to charitable, religious, civic, community, governmental and educational organizations in matters which are designed primarily to address the needs of persons of limited means.

---

4. Recognizing that broad-based participation in *pro bono* activities is desirable, our firm agrees that, in meeting the minimum goals described above, we will use our best efforts to ensure that a majority of both partners and associates in the firm participate annually in *pro bono* activities.

5. In furtherance of these principles, our firm also agrees:

   a. To provide a broad range of *pro bono* opportunities, training, and supervision to attorneys in the firm, to ensure that all of our attorneys can avail themselves of the opportunity to do *pro bono* work;

   b. To ensure that the firm's policies with respect to evaluation, advancement, productivity, and compensation of its attorneys are compatible with the firm's strong commitment to encourage and support substantial *pro bono* participation by all attorneys; and

   c. To monitor the firm's progress toward the goals established in this statement and to report its progress annually to the members of the firm and to the American Bar Association's Law Firm Pro Bono Project.

6. This firm also recognizes the obligation of major law firms to contribute financial support to organizations that provide legal services free of charge to persons of limited means.

7. As used in this statement, the term *pro bono* refers to activities of the firm undertaken normally without expectation of fee and not in the course of ordinary commercial practice and consisting of (i) the delivery of legal services to persons of limited means or to charitable, religious, civic, community, governmental, and educational organizations in matters which are designed primarily to address the needs of persons of limited means; (ii) the provision of legal assistance to individuals, groups, or organizations seeking to secure or protect civil rights, civil liberties or public rights; and (iii) the provision of legal assistance to charitable, religious, civic, community, governmental, or educational organizations in matters in furtherance of their organizational purposes, where the payment of standard legal fees would significantly deplete the organization's economic resources or would be otherwise inappropriate.

FIRM
PARTNER EXECUTING ON BEHALF OF FIRM
ADDRESS
CITY/STATE/ZIP
PHONE/FAX

Law Firm Pro Bono Challenge
Commentary to Statement of Principles*

Principle 1

Our firm recognizes its institutional obligation to encourage and support the participation by all of its attorneys in *pro bono publico* activities. We agree to promulgate and maintain a clearly articulated and commonly understood firm policy which unequivocally states the firm's commitment to *pro bono* work.

COMMENTARY
An Institutional Commitment

We ask that each law firm recognize and structure an active institutional commitment to *pro bono publico* service, rather than simply accommodating the interest and commitment of its individual attorneys. The goal of such institutional support is to ensure that the special resources and expertise of the firm are collectively focused on the management and implementation of an effective and productive *pro bono* effort and on the reduction or elimination of barriers to *pro bono* work. It is also designed to develop and nurture a firm culture in which *pro bono* service is a routine and valued part of each individual's professional life. The leadership of the firm should convey, in clear, unambiguous terms, the firm's commitment as an institution as well as its expectation that each individual will strive to help fulfill the firm-wide commitment. Many firms have found that a comprehensive written *pro bono* policy is an excellent vehicle for communicating that commitment. The firm should then implement its policy through a structured program that fosters *pro bono* work.

---

* © American Bar Association, 1993. Reprinted by permission.

Principle 2

To underscore our institutional commitment to *pro bono* activities, we agree to use our best efforts to ensure that, by no later than the close of calendar year 1995, our firm will either:

(1) annually contribute, at a minimum, an amount of time equal to 5 percent of the firm's total billable hours to *pro bono* work;

or

(2) annually contribute, at a minimum, an amount of time equal to 3 percent of the firm's total billable hours to *pro bono* work.

COMMENTARY
Quantifying the Commitment

We believe that the establishment of a concrete, quantifiable, firm-wide aspirational goal will assist firms in communicating support for *pro bono* and in assessing the overall effectiveness of their *pro bono* programs. The expression of that goal as a percentage of total billable hours, rather than as a goal of hours per individual attorney, underscores the institutional nature of the commitment. While we believe that it is both feasible and appropriate for major law firms to contribute 5% of their billable hours to *pro bono* activities, we recognize that substantial differences exist among firms with respect to their current levels of *pro bono* activity. Accordingly, we have provided firms with a choice between two alternative aspirational goals—a goal of 5 percent of total billable hours or a goal of 3 percent of total billable hours. Many firms already report contributions of *pro bono* time far in excess of either of these goals. Indeed, several major firms presently expend 8% or more of their time on *pro bono* activities. For other firms, accepting the challenge to aspire to even the lower of the two goals represents a dramatic expansion of their current level of effort. These levels are consonant with existing aspirational bar resolutions which call for annual goals of up to 80 hours per attorney. For example, we anticipate that the 3% aspirational goal will translate into a per-attorney goal somewhat in excess of 50 hours annually, a commitment that is consistent with the aspirational goals established by the American Bar Association and many state and local bar associations. Many major law firms have established branch offices in foreign countries. Recognizing that *pro bono* service may not be feasible for attorneys in these offices, the 5%/3% goals should be applied only to the total billable hours performed by firm attorneys working in the United States.

Principle 3

In recognition of the special needs of the poor for legal services, we believe that our firm's *pro bono* activities should be particularly focused on providing access to the justice system for persons otherwise unable to afford it. Accordingly, in meeting the voluntary goals described above, we agree that a majority of the minimum *pro bono* time contributed by our firm should consist of the delivery of legal services on a *pro bono* basis to persons of limited means or to charitable, religious, civic, community, governmental, and educational organizations in matters which are designed primarily to address the needs of persons of limited means.

COMMENTARY
Pro Bono—Meeting the Need

While we recognize and applaud the rich diversity of *pro bono* activities undertaken by law firms, with respect to the minimum aspirational goal established by the Challenge, we strongly support a special emphasis by firms on the legal problems of persons of limited means. Studies routinely report that more than 80% of the civil legal needs of the poor are not presently being met. The resources and expertise of leading law firms should be brought to bear to assist the most vulnerable of our citizens in securing their rights. Legal services, as used in this Commentary, consist of a broad range of activities, including, among others, individual and class representation, legislative lobbying and administrative rule making, as well as legal assistance to organizations seeking to develop low-income housing, improve community services, or increase the financial resources of persons of limited means. Many activities traditionally viewed by firms as falling in other *pro bono* categories such as civil rights or civil liberties cases, environmental claims, community economic development, and consumer protection matters can, in fact, often also be accurately described as falling within the priority for legal services to persons of limited means. Emphasis on the legal needs of persons of limited means is not intended to supplant the involvement of firms in complex *pro bono* matters for other populations. Many major law firms have a strong commitment to public interest litigation and projects, including high impact class action suits and policy advocacy, that promote essential public policies and ensure that our society functions equitably. Firms undertaking these complex and time-consuming matters often commit resources far in excess of the Challenge's minimum goals.

Principle 4

Recognizing that broad-based participation in *pro bono* activities is desirable, our firm agrees that, in meeting the minimum goals described above, we will use our best efforts to ensure that a majority of both partners and associates in the firm participate annually in *pro bono* activities.

COMMENTARY
Broadbased Participation in *Pro Bono*

While we urge the firm's institutional support for *pro bono*, that support will be enhanced if *pro bono publico* service is the concern of all lawyers in the firm rather than only a few highly committed individuals. Experience has demonstrated that broadbased participation at all levels, including the most senior members of the firm, is a key element in developing and nurturing a successful firm *pro bono* program. Myriad opportunities for service exist—opportunities that will interest and challenge senior partners as well as young associates, business and tax lawyers as well as litigators. Broadbased participation in *pro bono* service promotes firm-wide support for that activity and serves as a concrete and visible affirmation of the firm's institutional commitment. Finally, by involving lawyers with a broad range of interests and skills, the firm can enrich its service to the community.

Principle 5

In furtherance of these principles, our firm also agrees:

a. To provide a broad range of *pro bono* opportunities, training, and supervision to attorneys in the firm, to ensure that all of our attorneys can avail themselves of the opportunity to do *pro bono* work;

b. To ensure that the firm's policies with respect to evaluation, advancement, productivity, and compensation of its attorneys are compatible with the firm's strong commitment to encourage and support substantial *pro bono* participation by all attorneys; and

c. To monitor the firm's progress toward the goals established in this statement and to report its progress annually to the members of the firm and to the American Bar Association's Law Firm Pro Bono Project.

COMMENTARY
Promoting and Recognizing *Pro Bono* Service

a. We encourage firms actively to seek out a broad range of *pro bono* opportunities for their lawyers and to provide or secure the necessary support, training, and supervision so that lawyers will be encouraged to take on these cases or projects. *Pro bono* matters should be administered in the same manner as commercial work. All of the firm's resources and support services should be available to the *pro bono* attorney, and the matter should be subject to the firm's oversight and quality control procedures. It is especially important that all *pro bono* matters be supervised in a manner consistent with the firm's overall supervision requirements. One obstacle that often limits participation in *pro bono* work is the concern that a firm lacks sufficient substantive expertise in particular areas of law. Many firms have taken steps to ensure that the necessary substantive supervision is available by identifying experts within or outside of the firm or by providing or securing training for firm attorneys.

A number of firms have established a *pro bono* committee, identified an individual to serve as the firm's *pro bono* coordinator, or otherwise formally assigned someone in the firm the responsibility for ensuring that the firm offers interesting *pro bono* opportunities and supports its lawyers in undertaking *pro bono* work. A formalized structure for identifying, screening, and monitoring *pro bono* work strengthens the visibility and effectiveness of the firm's overall *pro bono* effort.

b.   In an era of increased expectations with respect to billable hours, receipts, or similar measures, a firm commitment to *pro bono* must include positive incentives to perform that work. Whether this takes the form of billable hours credit, receivables equivalent credit, or some other form of recognition for time spent on *pro bono* work will depend on the firm's existing incentives system. It is equally important that participation in *pro bono* work be identified as one criterion for positive evaluations and advancement in the firm. Many firms have developed systems to ensure that such evaluations explicitly include assessment of *pro bono* work. Firms have also established supplemental efforts to promote recognition of *pro bono* work, such as firmwide *pro bono* awards and bonus programs.

c.   As part of its institutional commitment, the firm should monitor its progress in meeting its aspirational minimum goal, as well as its level of involvement in legal services to persons of limited means, and should disseminate information on the status of the *pro bono* program broadly within the firm. To assist the American Bar Association in assessing the impact of the Law Firm Challenge on the availability of *pro bono* firm resources, the firm will also provide information to the Association. That information will be confidential and will not be released in any form which identifies a specific firm.

Principle 6

This firm also recognizes the obligation of major law firms to contribute financial support to organizations that provide legal services free of charge to persons of limited means.

COMMENTARY
Financial Support

The level of firm *pro bono* commitment identified in the Law Firm Challenge is not intended to replace or diminish a firm's monetary contributions to organizations that provide legal services to persons of limited means. The Challenge commitment is one of actual service and personal involvement in *pro bono* work. We strongly encourage law firms to continue and expand their financial support of legal services organizations. These organizations need both service and monetary contributions from major law firms.

Principle 7

As used in this statement, the term *pro bono* refers to activities of the firm undertaken normally without expectation of fee and not in the course of ordinary commercial practice and consisting of (i) the delivery of legal services to persons of limited means or to charitable, religious, civic, community, governmental, and educational organizations in matters which are designed primarily to address the needs of persons of limited means; (ii) the provision of legal assistance to individuals, groups, or organizations seeking to secure or protect civil rights, civil liberties or public rights; and (iii) the provision of legal assistance to charitable, religious, civic, community, governmental, or educational organizations in matters in furtherance of their organizational purposes, where the payment of standard legal fees would significantly deplete the organization's economic resources or would be otherwise inappropriate.

COMMENTARY
Definition of *Pro Bono*

The definition of *pro bono* contained in the Challenge, although somewhat revised, tracks existing policy definitions adopted by the American Bar Association, state and local bar associations, and many law firms. The definition ensures that the firm and its attorneys can utilize varied legal skills to undertake a broad range of activities in meeting their *pro bono* responsibility.

Activities under clause (i) of the definition clearly fall within the recommended priority for legal services to persons of limited means, as do some of the activities under clause (ii). In the vast majority of all matters, the firm's *pro bono* participation will be undertaken without a fee or any expectation of a fee. However, there are very limited instances in which the acceptance of a fee award will not disqualify a matter from inclusion in the definition of *pro bono*. Post-conviction capital appeals, for example, where firms contribute thousands of hours without compensation but may receive the limited fees available to counsel under the Criminal Justice Act, are clearly *pro bono* cases for persons of limited means.

Similarly, the award of attorneys' fees in an employment discrimination or environmental protection case originally taken on by a firm as a *pro bono* matter and not in the course of the firm's ordinary commercial practice would not disqualify such services from inclusion as *pro bono* work. Firms that receive fees in such cases are encouraged to contribute an appropriate portion of those fees to organizations or projects that provide services to persons of limited means.

Appendix E

Women in the Legal Profession Committee
Model Annotated Mentoring Policy

June 23, 1995

This Model Annotated Mentoring Policy has been adopted by the Women in the Legal Profession Committee of the Minnesota State Bar Association. It will be formally presented to the Minnesota State Bar Association for adoption in October 1995.

"Mentoring is a special relationship and it requires its own set of attitudes, values, and behaviors."[1]

I. Introduction

With the apparent "transient" nature of law practice today, attorneys are changing firms and firms are changing attorneys at a rapid pace. Unlike law practice 30 years ago, it is the exception today to have an attorney who stays with one firm throughout the attorney's career. This situation can make the development of a relationship of trust and loyalty among a firm and its attorneys very difficult. A mentoring program can remedy this and can benefit today's law firm and its attorneys in many ways: increasing the competence and skills of all of the firm's attorneys, engendering attorney loyalty, fostering collegiality among the firm's attorneys and increasing attorney retention rates. *Merriam Webster's Collegiate Dictionary* (10th ed. 1993) defines a mentor as a "trusted

---

[1] G. Shea, 1992 *Mentoring: Helping Employees Reach Their Full Potential* 28 (1994).

counselor or guide"; a tutor, or a coach. Id. at 726. An attorney's success in a law firm depends on that attorney being guided and coached by senior lawyers to "learn the ropes" and to become integrated into the firm's social, cultural, and client system. Without such guidance, the attorney often will not make the grade; that is, partnership or advancement remains out of reach, goals of professional competence are not realized or the attorney becomes so frustrated that he or she leaves the firm. While these relationships can and do develop independently of a formal program, for many reasons, including frequent turnover, a formal mentoring program can ensure that all attorneys have an opportunity to develop strong mentoring relationships within the firm, and thus prevent people from "falling through the cracks."

Until recently, a large majority of women and minorities have not received a sufficient amount of this guidance, now coined "mentoring." In 1992, the Women in the Legal Profession Committee ("Committee") of the Minnesota State Bar Association ("MSBA") released a video "Getting to the Fine Points: Gender Fairness in the Workplace,"[2] which examines, through a series of vignettes and interviews, the obstacles to professional growth and satisfaction experienced by many of Minnesota's women lawyers. In the video, the lack of mentoring of women lawyers is identified as one of the most serious obstacles to their development within their firms and within the profession. The charge of the Committee is "to encourage and enhance the success and professional satisfaction of Minnesota's women lawyers." In keeping with its charge, the Committee decided to look into developing a model mentoring policy to remedy this lack. After completing a survey of legal employers in Minnesota, the Committee learned that very few of them had formal mentoring programs and almost all those surveyed indicated they would be interested in receiving a model policy. As a result, the Committee established a Subcommittee on Mentoring ("Subcommittee") to develop such a policy.

The Subcommittee initially considered the option of developing a program aimed solely at mentoring women, but concluded that the potential danger of a stigma being attached to a program available only to a designated group would be very damaging to its effectiveness. The Subcommittee concluded further that a program including all attorney employees would provide an equal, if not

---

[2] Minnesota State Bar Association, 1992 *Getting to the Fine Points: Gender Fairness in the Workplace* (Video and Discussion Guide). The video is available for purchase or rental from the MSBA and provides an excellent springboard for discussion of these issues.

superior, benefit to the women participating in it. In developing this model policy the Committee also hopes to assist in implementing the recommendations of the Hennepin County Bar Association Glass Ceiling Task Force Report,[3] subsequently adopted by the MSBA,which call for the development of mentoring opportunities for women and minorities equal to those of their male white counterparts to remedy the current imbalance.

While the Committee believes that an important underlying philosophy of each mentoring program should be to establish increased employment and advancement opportunities for women and minorities and to eliminate the institutional barriers that, whether by design or impact, encourage discriminatory treatment of these groups, the Committee's aim throughout the policy is the creation of equal opportunities for all attorneys to succeed within their firms and in the profession. It is the Committee's [*sic*], that this model policy be used by all legal employers and cover all attorneys. All legal employers using this model will need to tailor the policy to fit their individual goals and personalities. Small firms, legal departments of corporations, public service employers or other legal employers may need to make additional adjustments to fit their individual needs. A small firm or legal department, for example, may not have formal committees, recruiting coordinators or practice groups, and these employers will have to make the appropriate substitutions in such cases. Throughout the policy the word "firm" is intended to mean all legal employers. Likewise, the term "partner" should be read as an attorney at a senior level within the legal employer.

A firm using this model policy is urged to consider carefully its needs and goals and to tailor its policy accordingly. A mentoring program will be only as successful as the time, effort and resources put into the program. Adopting an ambitious policy without supplying the resources to achieve it will have adverse consequences on the morale of the participants and may end up doing more harm than good. An area of particular concern throughout the preparation of this policy has been the conflict between developing a relationship of trust between mentor and mentee and the firm's need to know the information passing between mentor and mentee. This conflict is addressed in the section on confidentiality, but each firm should carefully consider its own position. In the end it will be up to

---

[3]Hennepin County Bar Association Glass Ceiling Task Force, Walking Through Invisible Doors and Shattering Glass Ceilings (1993) (report issued April 20, 1993).

the individual mentors to do their best to balance their obligations to the firm and their obligations to their mentees.

This Model Policy is presented as a guide to firms implementing mentoring programs—the provisions of the annotated policy should be reviewed carefully before adoption by a firm.

The existence of this model, while a good starting point for developing a policy, is no substitute for careful and thoughtful drafting on the part of the firm. Anyone who discovers errors in the policy or has suggestions to increase the utility of the model is urged to contact any of the following: Jennie A. Clarke at 612/334-8842, Marlene S. Garvis at 612/290-6569, Kathleen H. Sanberg at 612/336-3000 or Kent M. Williams at 612/338-4605. Sample mentoring policies also may be obtained by contacting the foregoing persons or the MSBA office.

The Subcommittee wishes to thank the following for their contributions in assisting with the preparation of this policy:

Office of the Attorney General
Best & Flanagan
Doherty Rumble & Butler
Dorsey & Whitney
Faegre & Benson
Larkin Hoffman Daly & Lindgren
Leonard Street and Deinard
Popham Haik Schnobrich & Kaufman
Winthrop & Weinstine

II. Committee Members
Subcommittee on Mentoring
Marlene S. Garvis, Jardine Logan & O'Brien, St. Paul
Jennie A. Clarke, Popham Haik Schnobrich & Kaufman, Minneapolis
Kathleen H. Sanberg, Faegre & Benson, Minneapolis
Kent M. Williams, Heins Mills & Olson, Minneapolis

Women in the Legal Profession Committee
Co-Chairs:
Samuel L. Hanson, Briggs and Morgan, Minneapolis
Michele D. Vaillancourt, Winthrop & Weinstine, St. Paul

Edward J. Bohrer, Felhaber Larson Fenlon & Vogt, Minneapolis
Tamara J. Byram, Lind Jensen & Sullivan, Minneapolis
Jennie A. Clarke, Popham Haik Schnobrich & Kaufman, Minneapolis
Marlene S. Garvis, Jardine Logan & O'Brien, St. Paul
Rachel U. Gibbs, Coon Rapids
Lisa R. Griebel, Cosgrove Flynn & Gaskins, Minneapolis
Bonnie L. Kleman, Mid-Minnesota Legal Assistance, Willmar

Corrine G. Lapinsky, Wilson—The Leather Experts, Minneapolis
Elizabeth L. Laroque, Legal Assistance of Olmstead County, Rochester
John T. Rebane, Land O'Lakes, Inc., Minneapolis
Kathleen H. Sanberg, Faegre & Benson, Minneapolis
Bruce J. Shnider, Dorsey & Whitney, Minneapolis
Thomas B. Tate, Tate Law Office, South St. Paul
Trevor R. Walsten, Maun & Simon, St. Paul
Eugene M. Warlich, Doherty Rumble & Butler, St. Paul
Kent M. Williams, Heins Mills & Olson, Minneapolis

III. Model Annotated Mentoring Policy

A mentoring program is founded on at least three premises: (1) an employee (mentee)'s chance of succeeding is greatly enhanced by the mentee's ability to develop early on professional and personal relationships with a more senior lawyer, (2) a mentoring program that is available to all attorney employees will promote competence and a better work environment overall and (3) a successful mentoring program will result in the delivery of superior professional services and an expanded client base for the employer. Once a firm has decided to establish a mentoring program, it must identify and develop the goals it wishes to accomplish and then design a policy tailored to achieve those goals. Set forth below is a discussion of the areas that should be addressed by the firm when developing a mentoring policy and implementing a mentoring program that will achieve the firm's goals.

The boldface items represent suggested policy provisions, which are then discussed more fully in the comments set forth below the suggested provision.

1. *Goals of the Mentoring Policy*

In adopting this policy, the firm hopes to create and promote equal opportunities for all attorneys to succeed within the firm. This policy is not meant to replace individual efforts on the part of each associate or independent mentoring relationships developed outside the policy, but to supplement these efforts and relationships. The mentoring program is a tool for the firm in assisting the mentee in the mentee's professional development to the benefit of both the mentee and the firm.

COMMENT: Defining the goals of the mentoring policy is essential to successful implementation of a mentoring program. As discussed above, there are many potential benefits to be derived from a formal mentoring program. It is important that the firm focus on why the program is being implemented and what it is intended to accomplish in order to tailor the policy to achieve the goals most important to the firm. In most cases, firms will want to achieve multiple goals and many of these goals will overlap in the components of the program. At times, these goals may conflict with each other in dictating how the program will be structured (for example, in the conflict between the need for confidentiality of communications between mentor and mentee and the need for the firm to receive information about the mentee). The goals of the firm will affect all aspects of the policy, including the duration, the amount and nature of the financial and time commitments needed and the obligations of the mentors. In adopting each of the provisions of its mentoring policy, the firm should keep its goals and priorities in mind.

To facilitate discussion of program options, we have defined four primary goals that we have identified as the primary functions of a mentor. Where there is a difference in the program requirements to achieve different goals, alternative suggestions may be identified by capital letters following the section reference. A firm may identify with a goal as presented, but it also may need to tailor the goal to meet its own needs.

The goals of the mentoring program are:

1.1 *Integration*. To assist new or lateral attorneys in making the transition into the firm from law school or previous employment.

COMMENT: Integrating new and lateral attorneys into the firm, establishing a connection between the mentee and the rest of the firm and making sure the mentee has the basic knowledge of the firm and its operations needed to get work done are important functions of the mentoring program because the mentee's connection to the firm will be established primarily within the first few months of employment. Starting with a new firm, however desirable the position, is a stressful and traumatic time. Each mentee will need the support of the mentor in making this transition.

Mentees who do not receive sufficient support in making the transition may find themselves feeling isolated, discontented and alienated. Recognizing the importance of this transition period, many firms already have orientation programs in existence. An orientation program of some length is essential to give the new attorney basic information about the firm and its operations. Firms with existing orientation programs may integrate their programs into the mentoring program, but at a minimum they must coordinate the two programs so they are not working at cross purposes.

1.2 *Training*. To facilitate the professional training, skills, and development of technical competence of the firm's attorneys.

COMMENT: This goal is viewed as one of the most significant direct benefits of a mentoring program to a firm. This goal most directly affects increasing the technical competence of the mentees, but it also promotes collegiality, loyalty and retention.

1.3 *Resource*. For the mentor to serve as a source of information and referrals to the mentee with respect to firm, legal, client, and community information.

COMMENT: This goal reflects the important function of the mentor as a door the mentee may knock on as a source of information (or direction as to where to obtain information) on matters that may range from completing time sheets, to direction on a research project, to information about a particular judge or client.

1.4 *Advisor*. For the mentor to act as advisor and confidante to the mentee to assist the mentee in the mentee's career and professional development, development of professional and personal relationships in and out of the firm, and the resolution of professional and, as appropriate, personal problems that may develop.

COMMENT: Most firms will be very comfortable with mentoring programs tailored to achieve the first three goals. It is in considering whether and how far to go in adopting this fourth goal, however, that many difficult issues will arise because of the nature of the relationship to be created between the mentor and the mentee and the additional obligations of the mentor and mentee to achieve this relationship. In adopting this goal, the other goals essentially may become subsets because they all represent means to assist the development and advancement of the mentee within the firm. A mentoring program should be uniquely suited to evolve with the mentee and to help provide the mentee with the tools needed to advance within the firm. To be successful, the mentee needs to be trained not only in areas of technical competence but also in marketing, firm politics, client servicing, and client development. The mentor will provide this training, serve to create a connection between the mentee and the firm and provide an on-going support mechanism for the mentee, ideally both professionally and personally, to assist in resolution of problems and to provide early warning of problems as they may arise. The mentor should assist the mentee in all aspects of career and professional development.

2. General Provisions

2.1 All [FILL IN APPROPRIATE CLASSES, LEVELS OR POSITIONS, e.g. associates, newly-hired attorneys] will be eligible and required to participate in the program for its duration.

COMMENT: All attorneys of the described levels should be required to participate in the program. Some firms, however, may desire to make the program optional or to allow an attorney to opt out after a set period of time. This is not recommended because the goals of the program may not be achieved for any attorney not participating, or a class of non-participating attorneys may develop which may, depending on the nature of the group, result in a stigma being attached to participants. Depending on the duration or other structural requirements of the program, currently employed or lateral attorneys may be of a seniority beyond the program. All new hires will need to be integrated into the firm and learn its procedures and practices, however, so it is recommended that the program be structured to include participation by all lateral hires.

2.2 Mentors will be selected from volunteering partners.

COMMENT: Participation by mentors, unlike mentees, must be voluntary. Mentors should want to contribute their time to the program. The mentor's commitment to the program is vital to its success. Mentoring requires a substantial commitment of time and effort; thus, all participants must be diligent, conscientious participants. In certain situations, it may be appropriate to use senior associates as mentors for certain aspects of the program, such as training, orientation, or until the mentee reaches a certain level of seniority. Firms also should not overlook their retired partners and of counsel as potential mentors. The value to the mentees of contact with active partners at an early stage in their professional development, however, should not be overlooked.

2.3 Mentors will receive [FILL IN APPROPRIATE BENEFIT OR PAYMENT, e.g. credit toward billable hour requirements] for participating in the program.

COMMENT: The mentoring program will be only as successful as the commitment and efforts of the mentors. The partnership must commit sufficient time and resources to make it succeed. Incentives and benefits of some type should be given to mentors to reward participation and to recognize the value to the firm of developing one of its most valuable resources. Possibilities include a reduction in other requirements or responsibilities—such as hourly or billing levels, set monetary bonuses, or billing or hourly credits. These benefits may be predicated on satisfactory performance of the mentor's duties and may be taken away if the mentor does not perform adequately.

2.4 The budget for the mentoring program will be sufficient to accomplish the goals of the program. Each mentor may spend up to [$_] monthly for meetings with his or her mentee. Expenses to meet

individual needs of mentees, such as specialized training, will be approved by the mentoring committee at the request of the mentor.

COMMENT: For the mentoring program to succeed, the firm also needs to commit sufficient financial resources to accomplish its goals. Many firms set dollar guidelines for meals, depending on the purpose. Others provide a set amount and allow the mentor to spend it at the mentor's discretion. Firms should designate separate funds for (i) social activities designed to assist in integrating the mentee and developing the relationship between the mentee and the mentor and (ii) substantive needs of the mentee, such as additional training or seminars that the mentor and mentee may determine are necessary or advisable for training, developing a specialty, marketing purposes, or otherwise assisting the mentee's advancement in the firm.

2.5 The firm will provide training sessions for the mentors.

COMMENT: The mentors—their quality and commitment to the success of the program—are the key component to the success of the program. Effective mentoring is a skill, which, like any skill, can be developed with effective training. Mentoring is a growing area and there are now many consulting firms that can assist with the development of mentoring programs and the training of the mentors. Training in sensitivity to diversity issues also is an important aspect of training mentors.

2.6 The firm will conduct an orientation session for new mentees to explain the provisions of the policy, the mentee's obligations, the mentor's obligations, and the method for requesting a change in mentors if it becomes advisable.

COMMENT: Effective use of the program by the mentees will increase its effectiveness. Communicating to the mentees their obligations in making the program work and giving them a clear sense of what they may expect from their mentors is important. An orientation session will ensure that mentees hear a consistent message regarding the program and give them responsibility for participating actively from the outset.

3. Oversight

3.1 The [FILL IN APPROPRIATE NAME, TITLE OR COMMITTEE, e.g. mentoring committee] will be responsible for the implementation, administration, and oversight of the mentoring program.

COMMENT: Effective oversight is a fundamental requirement for an effective mentoring program. The mentoring program cannot "run by itself," but rather it must be monitored, evaluated, and amended where necessary. In addition, the program manager must take care of day-to-day issues that arise, such as ineffective mentor-mentee assignments, recruitment and training of mentors and matching new attorneys with a mentor. The program manager also should have the power to delegate assignments with respect to implementing various aspects of the program. For example, the legal personnel committee might be assigned the ultimate responsibility for the program, but may decide the recruiting coordinator or the department heads should be responsible for matching mentors and mentees. It is important that the managers of the program be actively involved in assessing the progress of and making improvements to the program. The Committee recommends that the firm establish a mentoring committee (or subcommittee) whose sole function is to implement the mentoring policy. Other possible choices for oversight (in no particular order) include: human resources coordinator, management committee, recruiting coordinator, managing partner, department heads, practice groups, an individual partner with an interest in the area, personnel committee and/or mentoring committee. Firms also should consider giving the program manager the power to take away benefits from mentors who fail to perform their duties.

4. Duration

4.1 Participation in the mentoring program by the mentee shall last for [FILL IN DURATION, e.g. 1 year, 2 years, until partnership].

COMMENT: The mentoring program must be of sufficient duration to accomplish the goals of the program. The Committee recommends that a mentee's participation in the program last for at least two years. Programs focused on orientation of the mentee to the firm may be of shorter duration, but the Committee recommends that a mentee's participation in the program be no shorter than one year. Participation for a longer period is advisable if the goal is the advancement of the mentees to partnership (or its equivalent). As the mentee progresses in seniority, the need for a mentor may be crucial to assist the associate's advancement in the firm. In a longer program, the mentor may be rotated after two years, which will have the benefit of providing the mentee with contact with additional partners after having established what should be a continuing relationship with the previous mentor even after the "official" mentoring relationship has ended.

5. Matching

5.1 The matching of mentors and mentees should be done by a person or committee who knows the personalities of both lawyers sufficiently to make an effective match.

COMMENT: Time must be spent making good matches of mentors and mentees. Possible choices for responsibility in making matches are the recruiting coordinator, hiring partner, personnel committee, or department heads. It is essential that both mentors and mentees be able to request a change in mentors from the responsible party and that such change be done as diplomatically as possible to avoid recrimination or ill will. In addition, the number of mentees assigned to one mentor should be limited, ideally, to no more than two (2). Other options include selection of mentor by mentee or an initial short-term match followed by a long-term mentor chosen by the mentee.

5.2A The mentor need not be in the same practice area as the mentee. OR

5.2B The mentor should be in the same practice area as the mentee.

COMMENT: In the area of training, a mentor in the same practice area will be in a better position to assist the mentee with training in that practice area. If the mentor is not in the same practice area as the mentee, the mentor should make an effort to assist the mentee in discovering appropriate resources in his or her practice area.

6. *Confidentiality*

COMMENT: Any express obligations of the mentor to report to the firm should be communicated to the mentees so they may be aware of this obligation prior to making confidences. If the firm wishes to place an obligation on the mentor to come forward affirmatively with any specific information, that obligation should be explicitly addressed. Firms should consider explicitly addressing areas of particular concern, such as situations in which a mentee asks for advice in situations involving malpractice, sexual harassment, chemical dependency, or other sensitive areas that may involve potential liability of the firm.

6.1.A Firms will respect the confidentiality of communications between mentor and mentee, particularly in the conduct of mentee evaluations.

6.1.B Mentors and mentees will respect the private nature of the communications that take place in the context of the mentoring relationship. In the event the mentor (or mentee) learns information the disclosure of which is clearly obligated by law, the rules of professional conduct, or a clearly defined policy of the firm, the mentor (or mentee) is obligated to communicate such information to the appropriate person(s) in the firm. In the event disclosure is required, the

mentor should notify the mentee prior to disclosing the information and make every effort to keep disclosure of the information limited on a "need to know" basis.

6.1.C With respect to information learned by the mentor, the confidentiality of the mentor-mentee relationship is subject to the mentor's obligation to the firm.

COMMENT: Conflicts may develop for the mentor between the mentor's relationship to the firm and the mentor's relationship to the mentee. The policy should be carefully drafted to assist the mentor in resolving conflicts in difficult situations. This potential conflict will be most acute in developing an advisor-type relationship because it requires a high level of trust and a lack of confidentiality in the relationship will inhibit its development. The Committee, in wrestling with this issue, has concluded that the firm must respect the confidentiality of the relationship, particularly in the context of the evaluation of the mentee, for the protection of both the mentor and mentee. The mentor and mentee must respect the private nature of the information they may receive in the course of the mentoring relationship, except in clearly defined situations in which the knowledge of the mentor (or mentee) of a violation of law, the rules of professional conduct or a clearly defined policy of the firm requires that the mentor (or mentee) communicate this information to the appropriate persons. Similarly, it must be left to the individual mentor's judgment as to how and when third parties should be involved to benefit the mentee. For example, if the mentor should discover a substance abuse problem in the course of the mentoring relationship, it may become necessary in the mentor's judgment to involve someone else to obtain the assistance the mentee may require to resolve the problem. In the event the mentor believes information must be communicated to a third party, the mentor should inform the mentee in advance of this incipient disclosure and the mentor should make every effort to limit the disclosure to those who need to know. Each situation will be different, so it is difficult to give hard and fast rules—for each situation warranting confidentiality, one can develop a similar scenario where disclosure is needed. This is an area where mentors and mentees need to be very sensitive to the issues involved. Any training or orientation provided the mentors and mentees should include a discussion of this area.

7. Obligations of the Mentor

COMMENT: Each mentoring policy should define what is expected of the participating mentors. The more specific the requirement (e.g. meet a minimum of once a month for one hour) the more likely it is to be followed and the easier compliance will be to measure. In most cases, each of the obligations of the mentor will be applicable to the achievement of many, if not all, of the various goals. It may appear that the obligations of the mentor are more numerous than those of the mentee. This is a result of attempting to quantify and detail the tasks of the mentor and give mentors direction in achieving the goals of the program. The mentee is responsible for the mentee's own career and thus a mentee's obligations in that regard are much the same whether or not there is a mentoring program. The mentoring program is a tool for the firm in assisting the mentee in the mentee's development to the benefit of both the mentee and the firm.

The following provisions (Sections 7.1 to 7.10) are recommended for all policies:

7.1 The mentor should coordinate welcoming activities for the mentee's first day and meet daily for the first week, weekly for the first three months, and monthly thereafter.

COMMENT: Frequent and regular meetings are essential for success. The most crucial time for establishing a good mentoring relationship is within the first three months of the mentee's employment. If the mentee is not integrated into the firm during this time, feelings of disorientation, isolation and alienation may develop. The daily meetings in the first week should last for a minimum of 15 minutes, the weekly meetings in the first three months for a minimum of 30 minutes and the monthly meetings thereafter for a minimum of one hour. Frequency of meetings, focus, flexibility and shared responsibility are among the most important attributes of the mentoring relationship.

7.2 The mentor should be available as needed to provide advice and assistance to the mentee.

COMMENT: The type and scope of advice and assistance may vary depending on the goal of the program, but availability, assistance and advice are the heart of the mentoring relationship. Studies of mentees have found that patience, tolerance, and accessibility are among the most important attributes of a mentor.

7.3 The mentor should monitor the mentee's workload and assist the mentee in obtaining sufficient and fulfilling work or reducing his or her workload, as needed.

COMMENT: One of the key skills a mentee will need to develop is the ability to balance the mentee's workload. The mentor should be aware of the mentee's assignments and assist in obtaining work, if needed, or shifting work if the mentee is overburdened.

The mentor should assist the mentee in obtaining suitable and sufficient assignments. The mentor may include the mentee in the mentor's work, solicit work from others, or advise the mentee as to whom to solicit for work. The mentor also should make sure that the mentee's level of assignments increase in sophistication and difficulty and provide an appropriate and increasing amount of client introductions and contact. The mentor should assist the mentee in resolving conflicts among senior attorneys regarding work priorities and when the mentee has an excessive workload. The mentor's assistance will be needed especially in situations where the mentee faces competing deadlines for different attorneys. The mentor should assist the mentee in resolving these difficulties and should intervene for the mentee if it becomes necessary.

7.4 The mentor is responsible for following up with the mentee to check the progress of implementation of any plans of action developed with the mentee.

COMMENT: In all mentoring relationships, the mentor and the mentee will be developing plans of action—skills checklists, career development plans, marketing plans, or directions for completing research assignments. One of the mentor's responsibilities is to follow up with the mentee to check on the mentee's progress in putting the plans into action and to provide additional advice and assistance, as necessary.

7.5 The mentor should serve as a resource to the mentee regarding the firm's policies, procedures, resources, and clients.

COMMENT: The mentor will serve as a resource to the mentee as to details regarding the firm's policies and procedures, such as billing, reimbursement, leave policies, etc. The mentor should direct the mentee to the appropriate sources of information. The mentor should introduce the mentee to firm clients and/or suggest or arrange for other attorneys in the firm to do so, particularly attorneys in the mentee's practice area and attorneys for whom the mentee is working.

7.6 The mentor should provide guidance or other appropriate assistance to the mentee in completing work assignments.

COMMENT: The mentor is an important resource for the mentee in obtaining direction on work assignments. The mentor can assist the mentee in deciphering assignments, complying with firm standards (e.g. in preparing memoranda) and suggesting alternate lines of inquiry, as appropriate. The mentor can be an important source of information regarding clients, other attorneys both inside and outside the firm, judges, agencies, etc. The mentor should direct the mentee to the appropriate people for information, if the mentor does not possess it, or assist the mentee in finding out the information. The mentor should assist the mentee in receiving any training needed to complete assignments and provide direction to the mentee. The mentor should assist the mentee in developing file management and client management skills and in balancing work, competing deadlines, family issues, etc.

7.7 The mentor should introduce the mentee to the other members of the firm, department, practice group, support staff, clients, etc.

COMMENT: Introductions are a key aspect of orientation and becoming acclimated. They also are an important part of developing contacts within the firm. It is important to the mentee to know who people are in the firm, both to know where to go to get work done and to seek out work to assist in the mentee's professional development.

7.8 The mentor shall recommend and assist the mentee in participating in firm training sessions, outside seminars, or other appropriate learning opportunities.

COMMENT: The mentor should make the mentee aware of training opportunities conducted by the firm or by others. The mentor also may need to assist the mentee in obtaining approval to attend a seminar, particularly one that may require travel out of town, or in arranging the mentee's schedule to have the time to be away from the office to attend the seminar.

7.9 The mentor should serve as a resource to the mentee regarding the legal community and the community at large, as appropriate.

COMMENT: The mentor should direct the mentee to legal organizations, such as the MSBA, HCBA, Federal Bar Association, MTLA, pro bono opportunities, Legal Aid, etc. Mentees who are new to the area may need particular assistance in establishing themselves in the community.

7.10 The mentor should arrange mutually comfortable meetings with the mentee to promote the personal and social aspect of the mentor's role, such as lunches, dinners, social meetings, and meetings off the firm premises. These may include the mentee's family, if appropriate.

COMMENT: The early development of professional and personal relationships within the firm is a very important factor in professional development and retention. To this end, the mentor should be responsible for developing a relationship with the mentee that has a social and personal context. The types of activities undertaken need to be appropriate and mutually comfortable to both mentor and mentee. The mentor must use good judgment in this area. To encourage this, the firm should support various types of activities, such as reimbursement for mentor-mentee lunches, providing sporting or cultural event tickets, etc.

The following provision (Section 7.11) is recommended for policies with the goal of training mentees:

7.11 The mentor should assist the mentee in developing a plan of tasks to be accomplished within a certain time frame. The mentor should work with the mentee's supervisor to ensure that the mentee is provided the opportunity to achieve the tasks.

COMMENT: Attorneys "learn by doing." An attorney must be provided a wide range of experience in order to have a well-rounded career. Thus, for example, litigation attorneys should know the fundamentals of drafting pleadings, reviewing documents, and taking and defending depositions, as well as arguing motions and negotiating with opposing counsel. The mentor should communicate with the mentee to ensure that the mentee is becoming accomplished in all the requisite skills within his or her practice area. Even firms with a separate training program will benefit from having a mentor following up one-on-one with his or her mentee to ensure that the mentee's training is complete. Some firms have developed "skills checklists" for each practice area to assist the mentor and mentee in this endeavor.

The following provisions (Sections 7.12 to 7.15) are suggested for programs adopting the "advisor" goal:

7.12 The mentor should develop a plan of professional and career goals with mentee.

COMMENT: The plan should contain both short-term and long-term goals. The mentor should assist the mentee in developing plans for work projects, specialization, client development, professional activities, and community activities, as appropriate. The mentor should be aware of the mentee's interests and how they fit into the long-term plan of the mentee and the firm. Some firms provide an outline of the areas to be covered by the plan in which the goals for the mentee and the responsibilities of the mentor in assisting the mentee are set out for each of the specified areas (such as marketing, development of a specialty, etc.).

7.13 The mentor should assist the mentee with the planning and performance of appropriate business development or marketing activities.

COMMENT: Business development and marketing activities are extremely important to the visibility and success of the mentee within the firm and can provide the firm with new clients and business opportunities. The mentor can be an important source of introductions, ideas, training, and support to the mentee in conducting these activities effectively and successfully.

7.14 The mentor should foster and encourage the mentee, act as the mentee's proponent or facilitator within the firm, and make every effort to "open doors" for the mentee in the firm, among clients, and in the community.

COMMENT: As part of achieving the professional development of the mentee within the firm, the mentor will be acting as an advocate of the mentee and be the representative of the mentee to the firm. This is not a guarantee of success, nor is it meant to encourage the mentor to ignore any problems in the development of the mentee, but rather it is a means to resolve any such problems early, if possible, and to make sure that the mentee is fairly represented to the firm.

7.15 The mentor should assist the mentee in resolving personality conflicts or other difficulties. The mentor should be alert to signs of alienation or discontent in the mentee and should take appropriate steps to help resolve any problems that arise.

COMMENT: In light of the mentor's relationship to the mentee, the mentor will be in a position to make early detection of any developing problems. If any such problems are brought to the attention of the mentor by the mentee or otherwise, the mentor should attempt to resolve them with the mentee, or, if appropriate and the situation warrants, with third parties. The mentor should be particularly sensitive to the confidentiality issues discussed in Section 6. Firms may wish to explicitly address a mentor's obligation in the event of situations such as substance chemical dependency, illness, or other situations that may affect the firm's well-being as well as that of the mentee. The mentor can serve as a sounding board or sympathetic ear to the mentee and advise the mentee as to firm culture and politics.

8. *Obligations of the Mentee*

COMMENT: The mentee's obligations consist primarily in sharing with the mentor the obligations of developing the mentoring relationship and in following through on plans developed with the mentor. The mentoring program does not relieve the mentee of the obligation to pursue all methods of career and professional development, but it serves as a channel to help direct those activities to the benefit of both the mentee and the firm.

8.1 The mentee shares in the responsibility of arranging meetings with the mentor.

COMMENT: The mentee needs to be proactive in developing the mentoring relationship, which may require the mentee to take the initiative in arranging meetings with the mentor. The mentee should seek out the mentor informally between meetings. The mentee shares responsibility with the mentor in developing a mutually comfortable relationship.

8.2 The mentee is responsible for following through on plans of action developed with the mentor.

COMMENT: The mentoring program is not intended to replace individual efforts by the mentee; rather it is to support, direct, and supplement them. The associate is responsible for managing his or her own career. The mentee must take advantage of the opportunities provided by the mentor and continue to act pro actively in the mentee's own professional development.

8.3 The mentee should seek out the mentor informally between scheduled meetings.

COMMENT: This is an effective way for the mentee to assist in the development of the mentoring relationship.

9. *Participation in Performance Reviews*

COMMENT: Each policy should address specifically the role of the mentor in reviewing the mentee's job performance—whether the mentor should participate in the performance review or not and, if so, the capacity in which the mentor will be participating.

9.1 The mentor should be aware of the contents of the mentee's reviews, meet with the mentee shortly after the review to discuss its contents and meaning and, if improvement is needed, develop with the mentee a plan for making such improvement.

COMMENT: Some firms may wish to have the mentor present at reviews to provide support to the mentee and to hear first-hand what is said.

9.2.A The mentor will not have a role in reviewing the mentee's performance on behalf of the firm, except for reviewing work done directly for the mentor by the mentee.

OR

9.2.B The mentor should be a resource of the law firm in evaluating the mentee's performance.

COMMENT: Before implementing either of these provisions, firms must assess carefully the priority of their varying goals for the mentoring program. If the mentor has responsibility for giving the mentee's performance review, this will seriously undermine the development of the mentoring relationship, except for relationships that are purely for training purposes. The mentoring relationship can be most hindered or harmed by a mentor who also has direct supervisory control over the mentee. The relationship will be more effective if the mentor does not have responsibility for reviewing the mentee's performance on behalf of the firm, except for work the mentee completes for the mentor. The mentor, however, may serve as an excellent source of information to the firm regarding the personality, progress and potential of the mentee. Ideally, the mentor will advocate on behalf of the mentee to the extent possible, act as a resource to report on the progress and efforts of the mentee, and suggest means of assisting the mentee to progress, rather than assessing the mentee against others at the mentee's level in terms of advancement. The mentor's obligations to the firm and to convey information regarding the mentee should be explicitly stated, particularly if they take precedence over any confidentiality provisions. Some firms have resolved this issue by having two mentors assigned to each mentee, one of whom serves the advisor function while the other focuses more on the training aspect and assesses the mentee for the firm.

10. *Evaluation of the Mentoring Program*

10.1 The mentees will be interviewed after three months to determine if the match is effective and if the mentor is performing his or her obligations adequately. If the match is not satisfactory, a change in mentors will be effected in a diplomatic manner.

COMMENT: As discussed above, the first three months is critical to the integration of the mentee into the firm's culture. If a solid relationship has not been formed by the end of that period, it is crucial to attempt to remediate the situation as soon as it is detected so the mentee is not allowed to become isolated or alienated. The evaluations may be done by the program manager or delegated by the program manager to other appropriate person(s) or committee(s).

10.2 Mentors and mentees will complete evaluations semi-annually as to the performance by mentors and mentees and the effectiveness of the program. Suggestions for improvements will be solicited and the program may be modified accordingly. If advisable, a change in mentors will be effected in a diplomatic manner.

COMMENT: The committee or person responsible for the program must be given the authority to implement changes to the programs based on the evaluations. In oral interviews as opposed to written evaluations, the evaluator will have a better chance to sense if a change of mentors or mentees is advisable.

11. LEGEND: [Firm] reserves the right to modify, change, amend or discontinue this policy at any time, or from time to time, in its sole discretion.

COMMENT: As with any policy governing the benefits of employment, it is advisable for firms to retain the right to change or terminate the policy at any time.

IV. Selected Bibliography

This is not an exhaustive list of the resources on mentoring, but provides a sampling of the various materials available on the subject.

Applebaum, Ritchie & Shapiro, *Mentoring Revisited: An Organizational Behavior Construct*, 13 J. MANAGEMENT DEV. 62

Brown, Start With Structure: Creating a Mentoring Program, 68 MANAGERS MAG. 16 (1993) (discussing drafting mentoring programs for insurance agencies)

Chao, Walz & Gardner, Formal and Informal Mentorships: A Comparison on Mentoring Functions and Contrast with Nonmentored Counterparts, 45 PERSONNEL PSYCHOLOGY 619 (1992)

D. CLUTTERBUCK, EVERYONE NEEDS A MENTOR: HOW TO FOSTER TALENT IN THE ORGANIZATION (1985)

Colburn, Mentoring Today, Diversity Tomorrow?, 37 EDN 81 (1992)

Cunningham & Eberle, Characteristics of the Mentoring Experience: A Qualitative Study, 22 PERSONNEL REV. 54 (1993)

Dalessio, Does it Work? What LIMRA Research Says About Mentoring, 68 MANAGERS MAG. 10 (1993) (Life Insurance Marketing and Research Association)

Edmonds, Rod, Young Lawyers Urge Renewed Emphasis on Associate Training, DRI JOURNAL 4 (1994)

Geiger, Measures for Mentors, 46 TRAINING & DEV. 65 (1992)

Geiger-DuMond & Boyle, Mentoring: A Practitioner's Guide, 49 TRAINING & DEV. 51 (1995)

Gibb & Megginson, Inside Corporate Mentoring Schemes: A New Agenda of Concerns, 22 PERSONNEL REV. 40 (1993)

Heery, Corporate Mentoring Can Break the Glass Ceiling, 71 HR FOCUS 12 (1994)

Hinch, Everyone Needs a Helping Hand, 22 PUB. MANAGER: NEW BUREAUCRAT 31 (1992)

J. JERUCHIM & P. SHAPIRO, WOMEN, MENTORS AND SUCCESS (1992)

Johnson & Scandura, The Effect of Mentorship and Sex-Role Style on Male-Female Earnings, 33 INDUS. REL. 263 (1994)

Knippen & Green, Developing a Mentoring Relationship, 29 MANAGEMENT DECISION 40 (1991)

K. KRAM, MENTORING AT WORK: DEVELOPMENTAL RELATIONSHIPS IN ORGANIZATIONAL LIFE (1985)

Laband & Lentz, Workplace Mentoring in the Legal Profession, 61 S. ECON. J. 783 (1995)

MARSHALL, THE PROBLEM OF RETAINING AND PROMOTING MINORITY ATTORNEYS: ONE PRACTICAL SOLUTION—A MENTOR PROGRAM (ABA Perspectives on Competence Series 1992)

Mathes, Corporate Mentoring: Beyond the Blind Date, 68 HR FOCUS 23 (1991).

MENTORING: A COMPREHENSIVE ANNOTATED BIBLIOGRAPHY OF IMPORTANT REFERENCES (W. Gray & M. Gray, eds. 1986)

Mentoring policies (unpublished) of: Doherty, Rumble & Butler; Larkin, Hoffman, Daly & Lindgren, Ltd.; Leonard, Street and Deinard; Popham, Haik, Schnobrich & Kaufman, Ltd.

Minnesota State Bar Association, Getting to the Fine Points: Gender Fairness in the Workplace (Video and Discussion Guide 1992)

Minnesota State Bar Association, 1990 Report of the Women in the Legal Profession Committee (adopted June 30, 1990 by the Minnesota State Bar Association General Assembly)

M. MURRAY, BEYOND THE MYTHS AND MAGIC OF MENTORING: HOW TO FACILITATE AN EFFECTIVE MENTORING PROGRAM (1991)

Parvin, Someone to Watch Over You, 141 READER'S DIG. 127 (1992)

Reid, Mentorships Ensure Equal Opportunity, 73 PERSONNEL J. 122 (1994)

Scandura & Viator, Mentoring in Public Accounting Firms: An Analysis of Mentor-Protege Relationships, Mentorship Functions, and Protege Turnover Intentions, 19 ACCT., ORGANIZATIONS AND SOC'Y 717 (1994)

Serant, A Guiding Hand Can Help, 22 BLACK ENTERPRISE 25 (1991)

G. SHEA, MENTORING (1992)

G. SHEA, MENTORING: HELPING EMPLOYEES REACH THEIR FULL POTENTIAL (1994)

M. ZEY, THE MENTOR CONNECTION (1984)

Appendix F

Gambrell Award Winners (1991–1995)

1. *Virginia State Bar (Course on Professionalism) (1991)*

This is a two day course on professionalism and the Code of Professional Responsibility, presented five times a year and required of all newly licensed members of the bar, including those admitted by reciprocity, within one year of attaining active status. The course aspires to impart the higher than minimum goals of professionalism through a series of lectures and workshops led by a faculty of the most eminent and respected lawyers and judges in the state.

The course text is divided into three major areas: a lawyer's relationship to the business aspects of practice; a lawyer's relationship to his or her clients; and a lawyer's relationship to the legal system in general. A course handbook containing introductory materials, course lecture outlines and various appendices is distributed to all attendees. The introductory chapter includes an overview of major disciplinary problems. The lawyer/business chapter includes sections on business development, fee arrangements, and handling client funds and property. The lawyer/client chapter includes sections on independence, loyalty, avoiding conflicts, competence, maintaining clients, terminating employment, and confidentiality. The lawyer/system chapter includes sections on duty to the court, obligation of good faith relationships with lawyers and other parties, and obligations to the profession and the community. The appendices include principles of professional courtesy, a review of the disciplinary process, procedures for the investigation of complaints, and various bar information.

2. *William & Mary's Marshall-Wythe School of Law (Legal Skills Program) (1991)*

A required two year program that includes six courses: legal research; writing and analysis; introduction to appellate practice; interviewing, negotiating, and counseling; alternative dispute resolution; and legal ethics. Students are divided into four working groups in a 16-member "law office" to represent a series of five carefully designed "clients," learning firsthand what it means and feels like to be responsible for the legal affairs of clients. Students plan a practice activity by considering the moral and ethical dilemmas they will face in the activity to at least as great an extent as they consider legal strategies and tactics. Faculty members serve as "senior partners."

3. Case Western Reserve University School of Law (Professionalism Program) (1991)

The professionalism program has five components: a first year orientation panel that provides students with the opportunity to meet other students and discuss how professionalism issues will affect them as law students and lawyers; first year professional responsibility problems that are presented in the context of each substantive course; first year speaker series (open to all students) covering topics such as the pressure of billa le hours and the ethical dilemmas of lawyers with clients and witnesses who want to lie; film series about legal issues followed by discussion; and student evaluations and planning for evolution of program.

4. State Bar of Arizona (Peer Review and Diversion Program) (1992)

This program has three phases:

    a. *Diversion Program* Cases involving office management issues may be transferred to a probation-type program, freeing up the formal discipline system for more serious offenses and providing education and rehabilitation for individual lawyers.

    b. *Peer-Review Program* Provides a network of trained "mentor" lawyers in eight districts across the state to contact and counsel individual lawyers who display rude, offensive, and unprofessional behavior toward clients, other lawyers, court personnel, etc.

    c. *Mandatory Professionalism Course* All new lawyers are required to take the course within one year of being admitted. The course will be taught by lawyers who are respected for their demonstration of professionalism in practice and who are knowledgeable about the issues involved.

5. Nashville Bar Association (Colleagues Program) (1992)

This is a new program wherein 95 lawyers have been divided into 12 groups, each of which has one lawyer with more than 20 years experience, one with 5–10 years experience and a third with 10–20 years experience. All other participants have been practicing law for less than 5 years, with the vast majority having started in the past year.

Group meetings are held monthly. The experienced lawyers are asked to share the traditions that are part of practicing law in Nashville, answer the practical questions relating to relationships between lawyers, pass along the values of the profession, and guide in matters of general professional concern.

6. Cook County Bar Association (Cook County Bar Association/Attorney Registration and Disciplinary Commission Liaison Committee) (1992)

The Liaison Committee seeks to provide preventative and curative assistance to help lawyers change their detrimental practice habits and to implement efficient office management systems. The Liaison Committee focuses on lawyers who are the subject of ARDC charges of multiple neglect or minor conversion or commingling of funds. The program format consists of a three part structure: The Liaison Committee; The Of Counsel Advisor; and The Expert Panel. All Liaison Committee intervention is initiated by referral from the ARDC. The Committee then assigns an "Of Counsel Advisor" to work with the lawyer, "Respondent."

To assist the Committee with problem cases, a panel of experts in the following fields is being developed: Career Counseling; Law Office Management; Psycho-Therapist; and Certified Public Accountant. The Of Counsel meets with the Respondent monthly to monitor his/her case list; discuss the respondent's progress with the assistance from the experts, if any; and to monitor how the Respondent is responding to or resolving pending ARDC complaints. The program handles approximately four respondents per year. To assess the impact of the program, the number of complaints filed against the attorney after involvement of the Committee is monitored for two years.

7. Georgia Chief Justice's Commission on Professionalism (Town Hall Meetings) (1993)

A series of ten Town Hall Meetings was held around the state to assist and encourage lawyers, judges, and legal academicians to come to a shared vision of the profession. The meetings attracted 673 lawyers and judges. Information from questionnaires from each meeting has been collated and compiled and will be used to focus breakout group discussions at the Fifth Annual Convocation on Professionalism in 1993.

8. Queen's Bench Bar Association (All in a Days Work) (1993)

An instructional video using vignettes and a study guide dealing with gender bias in the legal profession. The bar also presents training sessions to law firms and law schools and makes the tape available to other bar associations who wish to present it.

9. Temple University (Integrated Trial Advocacy & Professional Responsibility Program) (1993)

Students apply ethical precepts and evidentiary rules in trial vignettes, trial advocacy problems, a civil bench trial, three disciplinary hearings, a criminal jury trial and a jury trial involving a claim of lawyer malpractice. Each exercise contains both substantive and practical evidentiary and professional responsibility issues. The course materials for Evidence, Professional Responsibility, and Trial Advocacy are completely integrated. One hundred forty-four students are participating in this year's program. Over one hundred had to be turned away because of space limitations. Professionalism, as well as ethics issues are raised.

10. Maryland State Bar Association (Professionalism – Beyond the Model Rules) (1994)

This is a mandatory course for new admittees. A volunteer faculty of forty judges and lawyers present the one-day course each fall and spring. The course combines videotaped vignettes, workshop discussions and individual presentations to give a "nuts and bolts" overview of law practice, highlighting the lawyer's relationship with the court, the client, the community, and other lawyers. Seasoned practitioners provide practical advice on "real life" situations the new lawyer is likely to encounter, and focus on professional behavior. One of the goals is to create a "mentorship" environment that will continue into the new lawyer's career.

11. State Bar of California, Office of Client Relations (Educating Membership on the Importance of Good Client Relations) (1994)

There are a number of facets to this project, including the following: the bar has developed a presentation, "Good Client Relations: The Key to Success," which has been given over 20 times; the bar is working with six local bars to have in operation by July 1, 1994 a pilot program for the mediation of client-lawyer disputes; the bar is working with local bars to have local lawyers address community and civic groups on the nature of the client-lawyer relationship; the bar is planning to produce two videotapes, with accompanying written materials, focusing on developing good client relations and qualifying for MCLE credit in law practice management; and the bar has compiled a bibliography of client relations materials.

12. The American Inns of Court (AIC) (1994)

The Inns have adopted a modified British model of legal apprenticeship. Each AIC has four categories of members: Master of the

Bench—consisting of judges, lawyers and law professors with more than fifteen years experience; Barristers—consisting of lawyers and law professors with from three to fifteen years experience; Associates—consisting of lawyers with less than three years experience; and Pupils—consisting of third-year law students.

Members are divided into "Pupillage Teams," consisting of one or two Masters, one or two Barristers, and Pupils or Associates. Each team is responsible for conducting one demonstration a year, focusing on a particular segment of the litigation process. The presentations are followed by discussion and critique. Also, each younger member of an AIC is assigned to a more experienced lawyer and to a judge, as mentors and persons with whom personal conversations can be had about the practice of law. The younger member spends time with his or her mentor each month, in court, in deposition, or in the office, observing and then discussing what has been observed.

13. New Hampshire Bar Association (Professionalism & Management: Keys to a Successful Law Practice) (1995)

This program was designed for solo and small firm practitioners to learn how to professionally manage a law practice. It provides participants with comprehensive knowledge and practical tools to effectively manage their firms and serve their clients. The design and implementation of the program is a cooperative effort of the bar association, law school, legal administrators group and risk management insurance carrier.

The program is a series of six, four hour workshops focusing on professionalism and law practice management. The workshops cover: Starting and Operating a Law Practice, Business Planning, Practice Systems and File Maintenance, Lawyer/Client Dynamics, Equipment and Resources, and Making It Work in the Real World.

14. Seattle University School of Law (Professional Responsibility Integrative Component Clinic) (1995)

This program, run in conjunction with the Washington State Bar, allows students to investigate current disciplinary complaints. The clinic has a course room component where students learn about the disciplinary system. The seminar continues throughout the semester, focusing on the actual cases under investigation (confidentiality is maintained.) Students investigate, develop the facts necessary to make the probable cause determination and draft recommendations and "trial briefs" based on their findings. The program provides students a "real-world" understanding of the tensions and ambiguities of practice. With the cooperation of the Bar, the program emphasizes the educational continuum from law school into practice.

15. Law Offices of Goldstein and Baron (Family Law Clinic) (1995)

Set up within the firm to help alleviate the overload of cases that would otherwise be handled by the Law Foundation of Prince George's County, volunteer interns work under the direction and supervision of the firm's domestic relations lawyers. A firm lawyer signs all court documents and appears in court with the interns. Interns are given on-going training and are supported by the firm's legal assistants and support staff.

The Clinic has arranged with ancillary providers such as process servers and court reporters to offer their services free or at a discounted rate to its clients. Judges and Masters have also cooperated with the Clinic, hearing the cases early in the morning before the regular court docket.

Appendix G

Teaching and Learning Professionalism
Selected Bibliography and Resources

A. Books, Monographs and Articles

Aaronson, Mark N. 1995. *Be Just to One Another: Preliminary Thoughts on Civility, Moral Character, and Professionalism.* 8 St. Thomas L. Rev. 113.

Abramson, Elliott M. 1993. *Puncturing the Myth of the Moral Intractability of Law Students: The Suggestiveness of the Work of Psychologist Lawrence Kohlberg for Ethical Training in Legal Education.* 7 Notre Dame J. L. Ethics & Pub. Policy 223.

ALI-ABA COMMITTEE ON CONTINUING PROFESSIONAL EDUCATION. 1988. LAW PRACTICE QUALITY EVALUATION: AN APPRAISAL OF PEER REVIEW AND OTHER MEASURES TO ENHANCE PROFESSIONAL PERFORMANCE.

Ambrosio, Michael P. 1991. *The Path to Professionalism.* 21 Seton Hall L. Rev. 524.

AMERICAN BAR ASSOCIATION. 1991. THE REPORT OF "AT A BREAKING POINT," A NATIONAL CONFERENCE ON THE EMERGING CRISES IN THE QUALITY OF LAWYERS' HEALTH AND LIVES—ITS IMPACT ON LAW FIRMS AND CLIENT SERVICES.

AMERICAN BAR ASSOCIATION CENTER FOR PROFESSIONAL RESPONSIBILITY. 1986. A SURVEY ON THE TEACHING OF PROFESSIONAL RESPONSIBILITY.

AMERICAN BAR ASSOCIATION COMMISSION ON ADVERTISING. 1995. LAWYER ADVERTISING AT THE CROSSROADS.

AMERICAN BAR ASSOCIATION COMMISSION ON NONLAWYER PRACTICE. 1995. NONLAWYER ACTIVITY IN LAW-RELATED SITUATIONS.

AMERICAN BAR ASSOCIATION COMMISSION ON PROFESSIONALISM. 1987. " . . . IN THE SPIRIT OF PUBLIC SERVICE": A BLUEPRINT FOR THE REKINDLING OF LAWYER PROFESSIONALISM. 112 F.R.D. 243.

AMERICAN BAR ASSOCIATION COMMISSION ON WOMEN IN THE PROFESSION. 1992. LAWYERS AND BALANCED LIVES—A GUIDE TO DRAFTING AND IMPLEMENTING SEXUAL HARASSMENT POLICIES FOR LAWYERS.

AMERICAN BAR ASSOCIATION REPORT OF THE TASK FORCE ON LAW SCHOOLS AND THE PROFESSION. 1992. NARROWING THE GAP, LEGAL EDUCATION AND PROFESSIONAL DEVELOPMENT—AN EDUCATIONAL CONTINUUM.

AMERICAN BAR ASSOCIATION SECTION OF LAW PRACTICE MANAGEMENT. 1989. THE QUALITY PURSUIT-ASSURING STANDARDS IN THE PRACTICE OF LAW.

———. 1994–95. MENTORING PROGRAM DIRECTORY.

AMERICAN BAR ASSOCIATION TASK FORCE ON PROFESSIONAL COMPETENCE. 1983. FINAL REPORT AND RECOMMENDATIONS.

AMERICAN BAR ASSOCIATION YOUNG LAWYERS DIVISION. 1989. PROFESSIONALISM—THE REAL BOTTOM LINE.

———. 1990. THE STATE OF THE LEGAL PROFESSION.

Aspin, Marvin E. 1994. *The Search for Renewed Civility in Litigation.* 28 Val. U. L. Rev. 513.

Association of American Law Schools. 1987. *Statement of Good Practices by Law Professors in the Discharge of Their Ethical and Professional Responsibilities.* 1995 AALS Handbook 89.

At Issue: Professional Responsibility—Has the Rise of Megafirms Endangered Professionalism? 1989. 69 A.B.A. J. 38 (Dec.).

BACHMAN, WALT. 1995. LAW V. LIFE.

Bacon, Roxana. 1992. *Supreme Court Adopts Sweeping Changes in Attorney Discipline.* 28 Ariz. Att'y. 10 (Feb.).

Baillie, James L. and Judith Bernstein-Baker. 1994. *In the Spirit of Public Service: Model Rule 6.1, The Profession and Legal Education,* 13 Law & Inequality 51.

Baldwin, Richard C. 1992. *Rethinking Professionalism—And Then Living It!* 41 Emory L. J. 433.

BALL, MILNER S. 1993. THE WORD AND THE LAW.

Ballman, Jr., B. George. 1994. *Amended Rule 6.1: Another Move Towards Mandatory Pro Bono? Is That What We Want?* 7 Geo. J. Legal Ethics 1139.

Bastros, Robert M. 1985. *Client Centered Counseling and Moral Accountability for Lawyers.* 10 J. Legal Prof. 97.

Berger, Curtis J. 1989. *A Pathway to Curricular Reform.* 39 J. Legal Educ. 547.

Biden, Jr., Joseph R. 1992. *Equal, Accessible, Affordable Justice Under Law: The Civil Justice Reform Act of 1990.* 1 Cornell L. J. & Public Policy 1.

BINDER, DAVID A., PAUL BERGMAN AND SUSAN C. PRICE. 1991. LAWYERS AS COUNSELORS: A CLIENT CENTERED APPROACH.

Blumenthal, Allen. 1993. *Attorney Self-Regulation, Consumer Protection and the Future of the Legal Profession.* 3 Kansas J. Law & Public Policy 6.

Blustein, Paul and Stanley Penn. 1982. *Advice or Consent—O.P.M. Fraud Raised Question About Role of a Criminal Lawyer.* Wall St. J. Dec. 31, 1.

Bok, Derek C. 1983. *A Flawed System of Law Practice and Training.* 33 J. Legal Educ. 570.

Bok, Sissela. 1990. *Can Lawyers Be Trusted?* 138 U. Pa. L. Rev. 913.

Bowie, Norman. 1988. *The Law: From a Profession to a Business.* 47 Vand. L. Rev. 741.

Braithwaith, William T. 1990. *Hearts and Minds: Can Professionalism Be Taught?* 74 A.B.A.J. 70 (Sept.).

Brandeis, Louis D. 1905. *The Opportunity in the Law.* 39 Am. L. Rev. 555.

Brest, Paul and Linda Kreiger. 1994. *On Teaching Professional Judgment.* 69 Wash. L. Rev. 522.

Brown, Jennifer G. 1992. *Rethinking "The Practice of Law."* 41 Emory L. J. 451.

Buchaman, John C. 1994. *The Demise of Legal Professionalism: Accepting Responsibility and Implementing Change.* 28 Val. U. L. Rev. 563.

Burger, Warren E. 1993. *The Decline of Professionalism.* 61 Tenn. L. Rev. 1.

———. 1995. *The Decline of Professionalism.* 63 Ford. L. Rev. 949.

Burke, Debra, Regan McLaurin and James W. Pearle. 1994. *Pro Bono Publico: Issues and Implications.* 26 Loy. U. Chi. L. J. 61.

Burns, Michael. 1986. *The Law School as a Model for Community.* 6 Nova L. J. 329.

CALLAHAN, JOAN C. ED. 1988. ETHICAL ISSUES IN PROFESSIONAL LIFE.

Claifetz, Jill. 1993. *The Value of Public Service: A Model for Instilling a Pro Bono Ethic in Law School.* 45 Stan. L. Rev. 1695.

Clark, Tom. 1975. *Teaching Professional Ethics.* 12 San Diego L. Rev. 249.

Clarke, Catherine T. 1991. *Missed Manners in the Courtroom Decorum.* 50 Md. L. Rev. 945.

Clarke, Harold G. 1990. *Professionalism: Repaying the Debt.* Law Prac. Mng. 29 (May/June).

COQUILLETTE, DANIEL R. 1995. LAWYERS AND FUNDAMENTAL MORAL RESPONSIBILITY.

———. 1994. *Professionalism: The Deep Theory.* 72 N.C. L. Rev. 1271.

Conference on the Commercialization of the Legal Profession. 1994. 45 S.C. L. Rev. 875.

Covington, Robert N. 1969. *The Pervasive Approach to Teaching Professional Responsibility: Experiences in an Insurance Course.* 41 U. Colo. L. Rev. 355 (1969).

Cramton, Roger C. 1982. *The Current State of the Law Curriculum.* 32 J. Legal Educ. 321.

———. 1994. *Delivery of Legal Services to Ordinary Americans.* 44 Case W. Res. L. Rev. 531.

———. 1978. *The Ordinary Religion of the Law School Classroom,* 29 J. Legal Educ. 247.

———. 1985. *Professionalism, Legal Services and Lawyer Competency,* in ABA, JUSTICE FOR A GENERATION.

Crimm, Nina J. 1994. *A Study: Law School Students Moral Perspectives in the Context of Advocacy and Decision-Making Roles.* 29 N.E. L. Rev. 1 (1994).

D'AMATO, ANTHONY A. AND ARTHUR J. JACOBSON. 1992. JUSTICE AND THE LEGAL SYSTEM.

DIETEL, J. EDWIN. 1992. SUSTAINING LAW PRACTICE EXCELLENCE.

Dillon, Karen. 1994. *Can the Profession Save Itself?* 16 American Law. 5 (Nov.).

Dimitriou, Demetrious. 1994. *The Individual Practitioner and Commercialism in the Profession: How Can the Individual Survive?* 45 S.C. L. Rev. 965.

Drinin, Robert F. 1969. *Perspective Courses in the Curriculum.* 41 U. Colo. L. Rev. 416.

Duncan, Laura. 1994. *Bar Associations Stand at the Ready to Assist New Lawyers.* Chi. Daily L. Bull. June 27 at New Lawyers Section p. 1.

DVORKIN, JACK HIMMELSTEIN AND HOWARD LESNICK. 1981. BECOMING A LAWYER—A HUMANISTIC PERSPECTIVE ON LEGAL EDUCATION AND PROFESSIONALISM.

Edwards, Harry J. 1992. *The Growing Disjunction Between Legal Education and the Legal Profession.* 91 Mich. L. Rev. 34.

———. 1990. *A Lawyer's Duty to Serve the Public Good.* 65 N.Y.U. L. Rev. 1148.

———. 1986. *Do Lawyers Still Make a Difference?* 32 Wayne L. Rev. 201.

Eisele, Thomas D. 1989. *Must Virtue Be Taught?* 39 J. Legal Educ. 495.

Eldred, Tigran W. and Schoenherr, Thomas. 1994. *The Lawyer's Duty of Public Service: More Than Charity.* 96 W. Va. L. Rev. 367.

Elkins, James R. 1985. *The Pedagogy of Ethics.* 10 J. Legal Prof. 37.

ETHICAL ISSUES IN PROFESSIONAL LIFE (Joan C. Callahan, ed.). 1988.

Feldman, Heidi Li. 1996. *Codes and Virtues: Can Good Lawyers Be Good Ethical Deliberators.* 68 S. Calif. L. Rev. 885.

FINAL REPORT OF THE COMMITTEE ON CIVILITY OF THE SEVENTH FEDERAL JUDICIAL CIRCUIT. 1992.

THE FLORIDA BAR COMMITTEE ON LAWYER PROFESSIONALISM. 1989. PROFESSIONALISM: A RECOMMITMENT OF THE BENCH, THE BAR, AND THE LAW SCHOOLS OF FLORIDA.

Frankel, Marvin E. 1994. *Proposal: A National Legal Service.* 45 S.C. L. Rev. 887.

FREEDMAN, MONROE. 1975. LAWYERS' ETHICS IN AN ADVERSARY SYSTEM.

Galanter, Marc. 1994. *The Many Futures of the Big Law Firm.* 45 S.C. L. REV. 905.

GALANTER, MARC AND THOMAS PALY. 1991. TOURNAMENT OF LAWYERS: THE GROWTH AND TRANSFORMATION OF THE LARGE LAW FIRM.

GILLERS, STEPHEN. 1995. REGULATION OF LAWYERS: PROBLEMS OF LAW AND ETHICS (4TH ED.)

————. 1990. *Counselor, Can You Spare a Buck?* 74 A.B.A. J. 80 (Nov.).

Gilson, Ronald J. and Robert H. Mnookin. 1989. *Coming of Age in a Corporate Law Firm: The Economics of Associate Career Patterns.* 41 Stan. L. Rev. 567.

GLENDON, MARY ANN. 1994. HOW THE CRISES IN THE LEGAL PROFESSION IS TRANSFORMING AMERICAN SOCIETY.

GOLDMAN, ALAN. 1980. THE MORAL FOUNDATIONS OF PROFESSIONAL ETHICS.

THE GOOD LAWYER: LAWYERS' ROLES AND LAWYERS' ETHICS (David Luban, ed.). 1983.

Gordon, Robert W. 1990. *Corporate Law Practice as a Public Calling.* 49 Md. L. Rev. 255.

Haddon, Phoebe A. 1994. *Education for a Public Calling in the 21st Century.* 69 Wash. L. Rev. 573.

Hall, Timothy L. 1990. *Moral Character: The Practice of Law and Legal Education.* 60 Miss. L. J. 511.

Harrison, Mark I. 1992. *The State Bar Professionalism Course: Not a Panacea But an Rx for Improvement.* 28 Ariz. Att'y. 14 (Feb.).

Hartwell, Steven. 1995. *Promoting Moral Development Through Experiential Teaching.* 1 Clinical L. Rev. 505.

Haynsworth IV, Harry J. 1994. *Alternatives to Value Billing: A Response to Demetrious Dimitriou.* 45 S.C. L. Rev. 981.

Hazard, Jr., Geoffrey C. 1988. *Four Portraits of Law Practice.* 57 UMKC L. Rev. 1.

————. 1991. *The Future of Legal Ethics.* 100 Yale L.J. 1239.

————. 1994. *Certification Can Boost Right Conduct.* Nat'l L. J. A21 (Aug. 29, 1994).

————. 1994. *Size Creates Tension.* Nat'l. L. J. A21 (Nov. 21).

HAZARD, JR., GEOFFREY C., SUSAN P. KONIAK, AND ROGER CRAMTON. 1993. THE LAW AND ETHICS OF LAWYERING (SECOND EDITION).

HAZARD , JR., GEOFFREY C. AND DEBORAH L. RHODE. 1994. THE LEGAL PROFESSION: RESPONSIBILITY AND REGULATIONS (SECOND EDITION).

Hellman, Lawrence K. 1991. *The Effects of Law Office Work on the Formation of Law Students' Professional Values: Observation, Explanation, Optimization.* 4 Geo. J. Legal Ethics 537.

HEYMANN, PHILIP B. AND LANCE LIEBMAN. 1988. THE SOCIAL RESPONSIBILITIES OF LAWYERS: CASE STUDIES.

Hurley, John J. 1994. *In Search of the New Paradigm: Total Quality Management in the Law Firm.* 43 Emory L. J. 521.

ILLINOIS STATE BAR ASSOCIATION SPECIAL COMMITTEE ON PROFESSIONAL-
ISM. 1987. THE BAR, THE BENCH AND PROFESSIONALISM IN ILLINOIS:
PROUD TRADITIONS, TOUGH NEW PROBLEMS, CURRENT CHOICES.

Janoff, Sandra. 1991. *The Influence of Legal Education on Moral Reason-
ing.* 76 Minn. L. Rev. 193.

Jenkins, Joryn. 1993. *The American Inns of Court: Preparing Our Students for Ethical Practice?* 27 Akron L. Rev. 175.

Johnson, Jr., Alex M. 1991. *Think Like a Lawyer, Work Like a Machine:
The Dissonance Between Law School and Law Practice.* 64 S. Calif. L.
Rev. 1231.

Johnson, Karl and Ann Scales. 1986. *An Absolutely Positively True Story:
Seven Reasons Why We Sing.* 16 N.M. L. Rev. 433.

Johnstone, Ian and Mary P. Treuthart. 1991. *Doing the Right Thing: An
Overview of Teaching Professional Responsibility.* 41 J. Legal Educ. 75,
87–89.

Kagan, Robert A. 1994. *Do Lawyers Cause Adversarial Legalism? A Preliminary Inquiry.* 19 Law & Social Inequity 1.

KATZMAN, ROBERT A. 1995. THE LAW FIRM AND THE PUBLIC GOOD.

KEEMAN, PATRICK A., ED. 1979. NATIONAL CONFERENCE ON TEACHING
PROFESSIONAL RESPONSIBILITY, UNIVERSITY OF DETROIT, 1979—MATE-
RIALS AND PROCEEDINGS.

KELLEY, MICHAEL J. 1980. LEGAL ETHICS AND LEGAL EDUCATION.

———. 1994. LIVES OF LAWYERS: JOURNEYS IN THE ORGANIZATIONS OF
PRACTICE.

KILLOUGEY, DONNA M., ED. 1984. BREAKING TRADITIONS—WORK ALTER-
NATIVES FOR LAWYERS.

Kimerer, Michael. 1992. *Diversion and the Membership Assistance Program.* 28 Ariz. Att'y. 18 (Feb.).

Kissam, Philip C. 1986. *The Decline of Law School Professionalism.* 134
U. Pa. L. Rev. 251.

Kleinberger, Daniel S. 1989. *Wanted: An Ethos of Personal Responsibility—Why Codes of Ethics and Schools of Law Don't Make for Ethical
Lawyers.* 21 Conn. L. Rev. 365.

KRONMAN, ANTHONY T. 1993. THE LOST LAWYER: FAILING IDEALS IN THE
LEGAL PROFESSION.

———. 1987. *Living in the Law.* 54 U. Chi. L. Rev. 835, 861–76.

KUKLIN, BAILEY AND JEFFREY W. STEMPEL. 1994. FOUNDATIONS OF THE
LAW: AN INTERDISCIPLINARY AND JURISPRUDENTIAL PRIMER.

LAWYERS' IDEALS/LAWYERS' PRACTICES (ROBERT L. NELSON, DAVID M.
TRUBEK AND RAYMAN L. SOLOMON, EDS.). 1992.

LESNICK, HOWARD. 1992. BEING A LAWYER: INDIVIDUAL CHOICE AND
RESPONSIBILITY IN THE PRACTICE OF LAW.

Lilly, Graham C. 1995. *Law Schools Without Lawyers? Winds of Change in Legal Education.* 81 Va. L. Rev. 1421.

Link, David T. 1989. *The Pervasive Method of Teaching Ethics.* 39 J. Legal Educ. 485.

LINOWITZ, SOL M. 1994. THE BETRAYED PROFESSION.

LUBAN, DAVID. 1988. LAWYERS AND JUSTICE.

———. 1988. *The Noblesse Oblige Tradition in the Practice of Law.* 41 Vand. L. Rev. 717.

Luban, David and Michael M. Milleman. 1995. *Good Judgment: Ethics Teaching in Dark Times,* 9 Geo. J. Legal Ethics 31.

Lutey, Selmer D. 1992. *Diversion and the Law Office Management Assistance Program.* 28 Ariz. Att'y. 22 (Feb.).

Martyn, Susan R. 1989. *Peer Review and Quality Assurance for Lawyers.* 20 U. Tol. L. Rev. 245.

Mashburn, Amy R. 1994. *Professionalism as Class Ideology: Civility Codes and Bar Hierarchy.* 28 Val. U. L. Rev. 657.

Maurer, Nancy M. and Linda F. Mischler. 1994. *Introduction to Lawyering: Teaching First Year Students to Think Like Professionals.* 44 J. Legal Educ. 96.

Maute, Judith L. 1992. *Balanced Lives in a Stressful Profession: An Impossible Dream?* 21 Cap. U. L. Rev. 797.

Mazor, Lester J. and Donald B. King. 1969. *Perspective Courses and Co-Curricular Activities.* 41 U. Colo. L. Rev. 432.

McCarthy, Jr., David J. 1986. *Some Brief Reflections on Johnson and Scales, "An Absolutely Positively True Story: Seven Reasons Why We Sing."* 16 N.M. L. Rev. 607.

MCDONALD, LINDA L. 1993. LEGAL EDUCATION AND THE PRACTICING BAR: A PARTNERSHIP OF REALITY IN THE MACCRATE REPORT—BUILDING THE EDUCATIONAL CONTINUUM.

McDowell, Banks. 1994. *The Usefulness of "Good Moral Character":* 33 Wash. L. J. 323.

McKim, Aimee. 1994. *Comment: The Lawyer Track: The Case for Humanizing the Career Within a Large Firm.* 55 Ohio St. L. J. 176.

Melickian, Mark. 1994. *Is Efficiency the Most Valuable Service a Lawyer Can Offer?* 23 Student Law. 14 (Dec.).

Menkel-Meadow, Carrie. 1994. *Culture Clash in the Quality of Life in the Law: Changes in the Economics, Diversification and Organization of Lawyering.* 44 Case W. Res. L. Rev. 621.

———. 1994. *Narrowing the Gap by Narrowing the Field: What's Missing from the MacCrate Report—Of Skills, Legal Science and Being a Human Being.* 69 Wash. L. Rev. 393.

———. 1992. *Is Altruism Possible in Lawyering?* 8 Ga. St. U. L. Rev. 385.

———. 1991. *Can a Law Teacher Avoid Teaching Legal Ethics?* 41 J. Legal Educ. 3.

METZLOFF, THOMAS B., ED. 1994. PROFESSIONAL RESPONSIBILITY ANTHOLOGY.

Minnesota Symposium: Legal Education & Pro Bono. 1994. 13 Law & Inequality 1.

Modjeska, Lee. 1991. *On Teaching Morality to Law Students.* 41 J. Legal Educ. 71.

Moliterno, James E. 1991. *An Analysis of Ethics Teaching in Law Schools: Replacing Lost Benefits of the Apprentice System in the Academic Atmosphere.* 60 Cinn. L. Rev. 83, 104–181.

MOLITERNO, JAMES E. AND FREDRIC LEDERER. 1991. AN INTRODUCTION TO LAW, LAW STUDY AND THE LAWYER'S ROLE.

MORGAN, THOMAS D. AND RONALD D. ROTUNDA. 1995. PROBLEMS AND MATERIALS ON PROFESSIONAL RESPONSIBILITY (6th Ed).

Mudd, John O. 1993/94. *Academic Change in Law Schools: Part I.* 29 Gonz. L. Rev. 29; Part II *id.* 225.

———. 1990/91. *The Place of Perspective in Law and Legal Education.* 26 Gonz. L. Rev. 277.

Muro, Gregory S. 1991. *Integrating Theory and Practice in a Competency-Based Curriculum: Academic Planning at the University of Montana School of Law.* 52 Mont. L. Rev. 345.

Nash, Jr., Gordon B. 1991. *Volunteer Work Can Recharge Batteries.* Chi. Daily L. Bull. 8 (April 20).

NELSON, ROBERT L. 1988. PARTNERS WITH POWER: THE SOCIAL TRANSFORMATION OF THE LARGE LAW FIRM.

———. 1985. *Ideology, Practice, and Professional Autonomy: Social Values and Client Relationships in the Large Law Firm.* 37 Stan. L. Rev. 503.

NORVAL, MORRIS. 1992. THE BROTHEL BOY AND OTHER PARABLES OF THE LAW.

NEW YORK COURT OF APPEALS COMMITTEE ON THE PROFESSION AND THE COURTS. 1995. FINAL REPORT TO THE CHIEF JUSTICE.

Osiel, Mark J. 1989. *Book Review: Lawyers as Monopolists, Aristocrats and Entrepreneurs.* 103 Harv. L. Rev. 2009.

Painter, Richard W. 1994. *The Moral Interdependence of Corporate Lawyers and Their Clients.* 67 So. Calif. L. Rev. 507.

Peck, Jeffrey J. 1991. *"Users United": The Civil Justice Reform Act of 1990.* 54 Law & Contemp. Probs. 105.

Pepper, Stephen L. 1986. *The Lawyer's Amoral Ethical Role: A Defense, a Problem, and Some Possibilities.* Amer. Bar Found. Res. J. 613.

Pipkin, Ronald M. 1979. *Law School Instruction in Professional Responsibility: A Curricular Paradox.* Amer. Bar Found. Res. J. 247.

Powell, Burnele W. 1994. *Lawyer Professionalism as Ordinary Morality.* 35 S. Tex. L. Rev. 275.

Powers, William B. Winter, 1995. *Report on Law School Pro Bono Activities.* 16 Syllabus 10 (Winter).

Pound, Roscoe. 1964. *The Cause of Popular Dissatisfaction with the Administration of Justice.* 35 F. R. D. 241.

The Profession–Identity Crisis. 1994. 78 A.B.A. J. 74 (Dec.).

THE QUALITY PURSUIT: ASSURING STANDARDS IN THE PRACTICE OF LAW (Robert M. Green, ed.) 1989.

Rakoff, Todd D. 1989. *The Harvard First-Year Experiment.* 39 J. Legal Educ. 491.

Ramos, Manuel R. 1994. *Legal Malpractice: The Profession's Dirty Little Secret.* 47 Vand. L. Rev. 1657.

Re, Edward D. 1994. *The Causes of Popular Dissatisfaction with the Legal Profession.* 68 St. John's L. Rev. 85.

Rehnquist, William H. 1986. *The Lawyer–Statesman in American History.* 9 Harv. J. L. Pub. Policy 537.

Reisman, Andrew L. 1993. *An Essay on the Dilemma of "Honest Abe": The Modern Day Professional Responsibility Implications of Abraham Lincoln's Representation of Clients He Believed to be Culpable.* 72 Neb. L. Rev. 1205.

RHODE, DEBORAH L. 1994. PROFESSIONAL RESPONSIBILITY—ETHICS BY THE PERVASIVE METHOD.

———. 1994. *Institutionalizing Ethics.* 44 Case W. Res. L. Rev. 665.

———. 1993. *Missing Questions: Feminist Perspectives on Legal Education.* 45 Stan. L. Rev. 1547.

———. 1992. *Ethics by the Pervasive Method.* 42 J. Legal Educ. 31, 41.

RHODE, DEBORAH L. AND DAVID LUBAN. 1995. LEGAL ETHICS (2nd Ed.).

Richards, David A. J. 1981. *Moral Theory, the Development of Psychology of Ethical Autonomy and Professionalism.* 31 J. Legal Educ. 359.

Rose, Henry. 1992. *Law Schools Should be About Justice Too,* 40 Clev. St. L. Rev. 443 (1992).

Rosner, Seth. 1991. *Professionalism and Money in the Law.* 63 N.Y. State Bar J. 26.

———. 1993. *An Outside Opinion—Independent Ethics Counsel Can Provide Fresh Perspective, Save Money.* 79 A.B.A. J. 112 (Dec.).

Rotunda, Ronald. 1988. *Demise of Professionalism Has Been Greatly Exaggerated.* Manhattan Law. 12 (Mr. 28).

Salomon, Richard A. 1986. *Professionalism: Should There be Limits on Lawyer Zeal?* Nat'l. L. J. Special Section 1 (July 21).

SAMMONS, JR., JACK L. 1988. LAWYER PROFESSIONALISM.

————. 1990. *Professing: Some Thoughts on Professionalism and Classroom Teaching.* 3 Geo. J. Legal Ethics 609.

Sammons, Jr., Jack L. and Linda H. Edwards. 1992. *Honoring the Law in Communities of Force: Terrell and Wildman's Teleology of Practice.* 41 Emory L. J. 489.

Sandalow, Terrance. 1984. *The Moral Responsibility of Law Schools.* 34 J. Legal Educ. 163.

Saunders, Kent M. and Linda Levine. 1994. *Learning to Think Like a Lawyer.* 29 U.S. F. L. Rev. 121.

Schneyer, Ted. 1993. *Policy Making and the Perils of Professionalism: The ABA's Ancillary Business Debate as a Case Study.* 35 Ariz. L. Rev. 363.

Schwartz, Murray L. 1978. *The Professionalism and Accountability of Lawyers.* 66 Cal. L. Rev. 669.

SHAFFER, THOMAS L. 1991. AMERICAN LAWYERS AND THEIR COMMUNITIES: ETHICS IN THE LEGAL PROFESSION.

————. 1985. AMERICAN LEGAL ETHICS: TEXT, READING AND DISCUSSION TOPICS.

————. 1990/91. *Inaugural Howard Lichtenstein Lecture in Legal Ethics: Lawyer Professionalism as a Moral Argument.* 26 Gonz. L. Rev. 393.

————. 1987. *Legal Ethics and the Good Client.* 36 Cath. U. L. Rev. 319.

————. 1984. *Moral Implications and Effects of Legal Education or: Brother Justinian Goes to Law School.* 34 J. Legal Educ. 190.

————. 1981. ON BEING A CHRISTIAN AND A LAWYER: LAW FOR THE INNOCENT.

————. 1979. *The Practice of Law as Moral Discourse.* 55 Notre Dame Law. 231.

Shaffer, Thomas L. and Mary M. Shaffer. 1989. *Character and Community: Rispetto as a Virtue in the Tradition of Italian-American Lawyers.* 64 Notre Dame L. Rev. 838.

SHAFFER, THOMAS L. AND ROBERT F. COCHRAN, JR. 1994. LAWYERS, CLIENTS AND MORAL RESPONSIBILITY .

SHAFFER, THOMAS L. AND ROBERT S. REDMOUNT. 1977. LAWYERS, LAW STUDENTS AND PEOPLE.

Shestack, Jerome L. 1994. *Even Today, Abraham Lincoln Has a Lesson for Lawyers.* Chi. Daily L. Bull. 6 (Feb. 11, 1994).

Shön, Donald A. 1995. *Educating the Reflective Legal Practitioner.* 2 Clin. L. Rev. 231.

Silver, Jay S. 1994. *Professionalism and the Hidden Assault on the Adversarial Process.* 55 Ohio St. L. J. 855.

Simon, William H. 1991. *The Trouble with Legal Ethics.* 41 J. Legal Educ. 65, 66.

————. 1985. *Babbitt v. Brandeis: The Decline of the Professional Ideal.* 37 Stan. L. Rev. 566.

Starrs, James E. 1965. *Crossing a Pedagogical Hellesport via the Pervasive System.* 17 J. Legal Educ. 365.

STOVER, ROBERT V. 1989. MAKING IT AND BREAKING IT—THE FATE OF PUBLIC INTEREST COMMITMENT DURING LAW SCHOOL.

Swygert, Michael I. 1989. *Striving to Make Great Lawyers—Citizenship and Moral Responsibility: A Jurisprudence for Law Teaching.* 30 Bos. Col. L. Rev. 803.

Symposium: Community, Pluralism, and Professional Responsibility. 1995. Geo. Wash. L. Rev. 921.

Symposium on the Corporate Law Firm. 1985. 37 Stan. L. Rev. 271.

Symposium: The Future of the Legal Profession. 1994. 44 Case W. Res. L. Rev. 333.

Symposium: The Growth of Large Law Firms and Its Effect on the Legal Profession and Legal Education. 1989. 64 Ind. L. J. 423.

Symposium: The Justice Mission of American Law Schools. 1992. 40 Clev. St. L. Rev. 277.

Symposium: Lawyers as Storytellers & Storytellers as Lawyers. 1994. 18 Vt. L. Rev. 67.

Symposium on the Lawyers' Amoral Ethical Role. 1986. Am. B. Found. Res. J. 613.

Symposium on Mandatory Pro Bono. 1991. 19 Hofstra L. Rev. 755.

Terrell, Timothy P. and James H. Wildman. 1992. *Rethinking Professionalism.* 41 Emory L.J. 403.

Terrell, Timothy P. 1994. *A Tour of the Whine Country: The Challenge of Extending the Tenets of Lawyer Professionalism to Law Professors and Law Students.* 34 Washburn L. J. 1.

Thode, E. Wayne and T. A. Smedley. 1969. *An Evaluation of the Pervasive Approach to Education for the Professional Responsibility of Lawyers.* 41 U. Colo. L. Rev. 365.

Tunney, John V. 1975. *Is the Bar Meeting Its Ethical Responsibility?* 12 San Diego L. Rev. 245.

Van Praagh, Shaunna. 1992. *Stories in Law School: An Essay on Language, Participation and the Power of Legal Education.* 2 Colum. J. of Gender & Law 111.

Veasey, E. Norman. 1995. *Rambo Be Gone.* 4 Bus. Law Today 12 (Jan./Feb.).

Wassenstrom, Richard. 1985. *Lawyers as Professionals: Some Moral Issues.* 5 Human Rts. 1.

Watson, Andrew S. 1975. *Lawyers and Professionalism: A Further Psychiatric Perspective on Legal Education.* 8 Mich. J. Law Reform 248.

Weinstein, Jack B. 1972. *On the Teaching of Legal Ethics.* 72 Colum. L. Rev. 452.

Weistart, John C. 1987. *The Law School Curriculum: The Process of Reform.* Duke L. J. 317.

Wiseman, Patrick. 1994. *Legal Education and Cynicism About the Law: Practicing Ethical Jurisprudence in the Classroom.* 25 Cumb. L. Rev. 1.

Wright, Julian H. 1993. *Beware of the Adversarial Shield: Possible Roles for Christian Ethics in Legal Ethics.* 23 Mem. St. U. L. Rev. 573.

Wright, R. George. 1995. *Cross-Examining Legal Ethics: The Roles of Intentions, Outcomes, and Character.* 83 Ky. L. J. 801.

B. Videotapes

America Media, Inc., *Sexual Harassment, Is It or Isn't It?* Interactive video containing 14 short, dramatic sexual harassment scenes. Includes training leader's guide and guide containing background information, EEOC guidelines, and steps for handling sexual harassment complaints.

American Bar Association Center for Profession Responsibility, *Ethical Dilemmas and Professionalism.* 1989. Five videotapes with discussion guides. Each videotape has a short vignette exploring a particular topic (attorney-client relations, client confidentiality, conflicts of interest, independence of counsel and associate-partner relations) followed by a panel discussion of the issues presented.

The American Bar Association Commission on Women in the Profession & Queen's Bench Bar Association, *All in a Day's Work—Facing Gender Bias in the Legal Profession.* 1993. Videotape plus discussion and facilitator's guides.

The Chief Justice's Commission on Professionalism in Georgia, *Ethics and Professionalism.* Videobased training programs for CLE and retreat events. Four videos designed for one- to three-hour programs, with teaching manuals and participant study guides.

Klein Associates, Inc., *Work Plays™: Flexible Solutions to Sexual Harassment in the Legal Profession.* 1994. Videotape training program contains seven vignettes in the "gray areas." Facilitator's guide included.

Loyola Law School (Los Angeles). 1994. *Counseling the Family of a Corporate Client: Matt's Case* and *Ethical Issues in Corporate Representation: The Seaside Resort.* Interactive videotapes designed for use in law school ethics courses.

Minnesota State Bar Association, *Getting to the Fine Points: Gender Fairness in the Workplace.* 1992. Videotape and discussion guide. Covers mentoring, exclusionary behavior, gender stereotypes, and balancing work and family.

National Association for Law Placement, *A Firm Commitment.* 1991. Interactive videotape exploring racial bias in the hiring and retention of minority lawyers. Discussion and facilitator's guides.

New York University School of Law, *Adventures in Legal Ethics* (nine videos) and *More Adventures in Legal Ethics* (six videos). Vignettes with discussion guides, prepared by Professor Stephen Gillers.

University of Pennsylvania Law School Center for Professionalism, *Professional Responsibility for Lawyers: A Guided Course.* Also available through CCH, Inc. and ALI-ABA. Five interactive videotapes dealing with conflicts and confidentiality, representing a corporate client, conflicts of interest in corporate transactions, professional responsibility in pretrial litigation, and counseling and negotiation. Discussion leader's guide, a case study, and study materials accompany each videotape.

C. Other Resources

Robert C. Cramton. 1987. AUDIOVISUAL MATERIALS ON PROFESSIONAL RESPONSIBILITY. Although somewhat out of date, this monograph, published by the American Bar Association Section of Tort and Insurance Practice, contains an extensive annotated bibliography of films and videotapes dealing with various legal ethics issues.

Keck Center on Legal Ethics and the Legal Profession. Professor Deborah L. Rhode, Director. Stanford Law School, Stanford, CA 94305-8610. An annotated bibliography of legal ethics materials and a compilation of innovative ethics teaching programs are two of the projects being undertaken by this center.

University of Pennsylvania Law School Center for Professionalism. Caroline M. Simon, Esq., Executive Director. University of Pennsylvania Law School, 3400 Chestnut Street, Philadelphia, PA 19104-6204. Founded in 1987, the Center for Professionalism provides educational programs examining crucial professional responsibility issues using interactive problem-solving materials and techniques. In addition to the interactive video series *Professional Responsibility for Lawyers: A Guided Course,* described in Section B of this Bibliography, the Center for Professionalism is producing and marketing multimedia case-study professional responsibility modules intended for use in substantive law courses, and also conducts CLE programs on ethics issues for lawyers and law firms.